Such Are the Trials

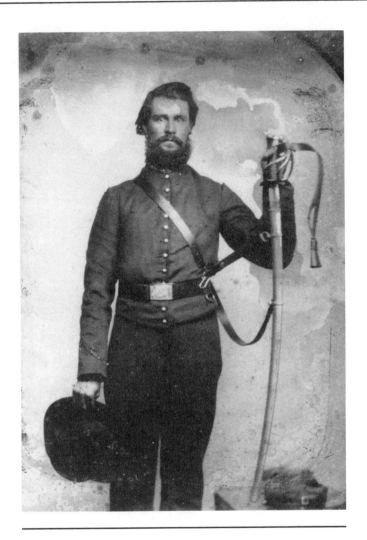

Jacob S. Gantz, Fourth Iowa Cavalry
1861-1865

Such Are the Trials

The Civil War Diaries of
Jacob Gantz

Edited by Kathleen Davis

Iowa State University Press / Ames

Kathleen Davis is a free-lance writer
and is feature writer for the
Texas Agricultural Experiment Station,
Texas A&M University, College Station, Texas.

© 1991 Iowa State University Press, Ames, Iowa 50010
All rights reserved

Manufactured in the United States of America
⊗ This book is printed on acid-free paper.

First edition, 1991

Library of Congress Cataloging-in-Publication Data

Gantz, Jacob
    Such are the trials: the Civil War diaries of Jacob Gantz / edited by Kathleen Davis. — 1st ed.
        p.   cm.
    Includes bibliographical references and index.
    ISBN 0–8138–0947–9 (alk. paper)
    1. Gantz, Jacob—Diaries. 2. United States. Army. Iowa Cavalry Regiment. 4th (1861–1865)—Biography. 3. Soldiers—Iowa—Diaries. 4. Iowa—History—Civil War, 1861–1865—Personal narratives. 5. United States—History—Civil War, 1861–1865—Personal narratives. I. Davis, Kathleen. II. Title.
    E507.6 4th.G36 1991
    973.7'81—dc20   90-48636

CONTENTS

PREFACE

When the Union and Confederate armies broke into full-blown civil war in 1861, the northwestern plains of Texas, where later I was born and raised, were then an unbounded prairie, the wispy blades of grass bending in unharnessed wind like the inviting curl of an index finger. They were the domain of Indians and the few cattlemen who could brave them on the dusty drives north.

Texans quite officially had voted on February 23, 1861, to secede from the Union and through the next four years would send some sixty-five thousand soldiers—about one-fourth of whom were killed or severely wounded in the Civil War battles across the South and along the Texas coastal bend.

But because there were few humans on the remote Texas High Plains at the time, it is safe to say that no ballots for secession were marked in that part of the state. More likely, the Indians and white settlers continued their own fatal conflicts with little concern about the divisive battles brewing elsewhere in the nation.

Yet in the years following the Great Rebellion—as civilization came to the flatland and vowed to exist in the arid climate with only the tall grasses and a sparse scattering of trees—the settlers bore the same awkward determination undoubtedly espoused by Dixie during the war: they were ill-prepared for what faced them but believed they were right; and they were willing to sacrifice with hopes of success. With the settlers came plenty of cottonseed and, unavoidably, their opinions of the Civil War.

Many of the early northwest Texas settlers had been in the

eastern portion of the Lone Star State during the four years of battling. Others, perhaps, migrated from the core of the Civil War's southern activity. It is anyone's guess whether the new settlers on the northwestern Texas plains were running from the ugly scars of a nation's bloodbath or were simply searching for a virgin region in which to again plant their cherished autonomy.

My hometown, Lubbock, is a relatively young city. Lubbock was only forty-six years old when I was born in 1955, and the Civil War had been history for ninety years. But I recall from my childhood that there was a sort of unspoken sentiment about the Civil War. Texas youths are taught in elementary school history classes that the Union blockade blistered our economy by halting the sale and shipment of the state's beloved cotton crop. And from that time, all the world's ills are blamed on the "Yankees."

Not that we new-generation native northwest Texans were supportive of the issues that led the southern states to secede. In fact, rarely were the issues debated at all. The pro-Rebel feeling, I believe, lent tangibility to the otherwise inexplicable degree of independence instilled in most Texans. As a child, I was apt to wave a Confederate flag or spout, "The South's gonna rise again." But even from my comfortable youthful existence, the stories I'd read of slavery ships and brutal plantations were revolting. As an adult, the song "Dixie" still moves me to tears, but so does the knowledge that more than half a million soldiers from both sides died and that once this nation I love was painfully split.

Easier it was, therefore, to profess my inherent love for the South but acknowledge no known ties to the actual conflict. That worked for more than three decades. But upon the death of my godfather and great-uncle, Harold Anderson of Watsonville, California, my mother, Jackie Harris, bequeathed many heirlooms. (Mother is a native Californian although she now has lived more years in Texas since marrying my sailor father in 1953.) It was there in a dusty box—packed among old pictures, books, and notes that would be dear only to our family—that she found the Civil War diaries of my great-great-grandfather, Jacob S. Gantz. The disquieting revelation, however, was that he wrote them wearing blue—not gray—as a private and corporal in the Fourth Iowa Cavalry.

Upon first reading the diaries—four hand-size volumes with daily entries from March 1863 until April 1965—I absorbed the words written by a stranger. Jacob Gantz was an unknown, after all. I had no affection for this man who long ago served the Union army. It ruffled me to read of cotton gins and southern cities being burned; it annoyed me to read Jacob's boasting that the "secesh skedadaled" upon the sight of the mighty Fourth Iowa Cavalry.

Perhaps Jacob's redemption in my eyes was his appreciation of the southern landscape that he recorded as if both to forget why he really was there and to remember what beauty existed in this land formerly unknown to him. With that in mind, I transcribed the diaries—faded and in some places blurred with the passage of more than one and a quarter centuries. And in doing so, I read again and again Jacob's words until I came to know him, to understand him, and, finally, to love him.

In July of 1988, I made a journey comparable in small ways to the one Jacob began on November 25, 1861. My stomach churned with anticipation as the plane approached Iowa. But I knew that my nervousness over visiting a land once his—a state I'd never been to—could not match the apprehension Jacob must have felt when he left his farm in Brookville, Iowa, bound first for Camp Harlan in Mount Pleasant, Iowa, and then to a southern land he'd never seen in peace much less in turmoil.

My first stop in Fairfield, Iowa—where Jacob lived after the war—was Evergreen Cemetery. Seeing his name etched on a tombstone, I felt, would be the physical connection between the man and his words; it would become real to me.

Beginning at the southeastern edge of the cemetery, I walked row after row reading all of the faceless names. It was after 6 P.M. and signs posted throughout the cemetery stated that no one was permitted on the grounds after dusk. Determination forced me on as the boiling sun inched closer to the Iowa hills. Within half an hour, I found a younger generation of Gantzes, perhaps of no relation. In another thirty minutes, I located the graves of Jacob's parents, which made me feel that he might be near. But after another forty-five minutes, with dusk on my heels, I was approaching the much older section of the cemetery and still hadn't found Jacob.

Dusty, hot, and tired from weaving up and down the hills and around the tombstones, I headed for a multilevel monument that had lingered peripherally during the search. It towered over the monoliths, the most elaborate family markers, and even a nearby mausoleum. A life-size, solid white Madonna stood atop the monument, hands clasped and glancing downward where—underneath her pedestal in an archway supported by four pink granite columns—perched the statue of a small female child. She, in turn, stood on a thick base of

Monument at Jacob and Louisa Gantz's graves,
Fairfield, Iowa.

white rock that had a large shell chiseled in each side. Under her, four more pink granite columns encased a squared and polished gray block. As I approached, I could see that the gray block was etched, undoubtedly, with remarks to commemorate some long-ago occasion. All of this—the two statues and gray granite block—was steadfastly stationed on two steplike slabs of concrete.

Leaning against it to brace my disappointment in not locating Jacob, I touched the age-worn etching about five and a half feet up the monument and realized the engraving spelled "Jacob, Louisa." Strange, I thought, that another couple shared the same given names as my great-great-grandparents. Then, sliding against it to sit on the base, I saw "4th Iowa Cavalry" and much larger, "GANTZ."

Dusk came as I cried and lingered with Jacob, Louisa, and two of their children who had died young. And when my tears had finished, I placed at the base a spray of silk flowers—yellow roses for Texas and white daisies like those that line my Texas lawn.

Maybe the waiting period of 125 years gave Jacob time to forget and me time to remember. I grew to love a man that I surely would have hated if I had lived in Texas during his life. He went to his grave proudly proclaiming his military involvement in the Union army; I went away from his grave proudly claiming my great-great-grandfather. Such are the trials.

Jacob left a diary to document his experiences in the Fourth Iowa Cavalry. Through it, I was privileged to come to know this man. Perhaps the reader of this book will develop both a deeper understanding of an ordinary man in the Civil War and a relationship with Jacob.

ACKNOWLEDGMENTS

This book started as merely my transcription of four diaries bequeathed from an ancestor. It was of interest only to my family, I thought. But as I talked to friends and relatives about Jacob's accounts, they began to encourage me to do more with the diaries so that others could share his experiences.

It is to all of those people, and to the many people whose paths I crossed in the resulting search, that I am so grateful.

One of the first to encourage, as always, was my graduate school professor Dr. Curtis Paulson, who now is at the University of Ohio. I also received notes of encouragement and bits of wisdom from a professional associate, Bruce Miles, director of the Texas Forest Service. Dr. Frank Vandiver, president emeritus of Texas A&M University and noted Civil War historian, sent me a much appreciated list of suggestions for research sources.

One of the first steps beyond my tedious transcription of the age-old diaries was to mail requests for information to Iowa and to Washington, D.C. The Iowa Archives in Des Moines made copies of several items they found on Jacob Gantz and mailed them to me free of charge. The National Archives was prompt and thorough in the searches I requested.

A highlight of this project was traveling to Fairfield, Iowa. Helpful assistance was provided there by a fellow journalist, Jan Nierling Bennett, editor of the *Fairfield Ledger*.

Fairfield itself was a comfortable place. I felt at home immediately and had not one unsatisfactory episode during my week there.

xiii

Everyone was as nice, friendly, and helpful as my neighbors in Texas.

Panic almost set in when, back home again, I discovered that I had failed to copy four key pages of a resource book that is unobtainable in Lubbock, where I lived at the time. However, Patricia Jennings at the library in Mount Pleasant promptly answered my request by sending the needed pages. That was a big help.

But I am most indebted to Verda Baird, a Jefferson County genealogist, who embraced my visit to Fairfield as if her own daughter had come home and who enthusiastically piled information in my direction leading me not only to a greater understanding of Jacob Gantz but also to finding another branch of my family tree. Thank you, Verda. Mrs. Baird has almost single-handedly provided a collection of genealogical materials in the Fairfield Public Library that will benefit many generations to come. It was a convenient and inexhaustible source for me.

To my many friends—who kept in touch and tolerated me through my hibernation with the word processor, who prodded me along, and who were convinced when I wasn't that the end would come, thanks.

And finally, to my parents and my two children, I am grateful that you put up with me through many hours of writing, that you shared my excitement with each new discovery, and that you offered your constructive thoughts on the topic. I love you all.

I

Introduction

W hen South Carolina became the first state to secede on December 20, 1860, Jacob S. Gantz and his wife, Louisa, had just begun a family with newborn son, Byron, on their farm near Brookville in Locust Grove Township, Jefferson County, Iowa. Quickly the rumblings of war spread. Within three weeks, the Confederates fired on a merchant vessel, *Star of the West*, and halted its intended delivery of reinforcement to federal soldiers at Fort Sumter, South Carolina. The Great Rebellion was steadily gaining momentum, and the Secesh (a term used in those days for a U.S. secessionist) early in 1861 chalked up several victories: the surrender of Fort Sumter on April 14; the abandonment of Harpers Ferry, Maryland, by the Union garrison on April18; and, the first Battle of Bull Run, a stream near Manassas Junction, Maryland, on July 21.

The threat of war must have seemed far removed to the young family nestled in the peaceful, rolling Iowa farmland. Gantz was one of six children—the second of four boys—and he had become an astute agriculturist.[1] But as Gantz planted and cultivated in 1861, the battles crept closer to his family's home front.

There were three Union defeats in neighboring Missouri: at Wilson's Creek on August 10, at Lexington on August 20, and at Belmont on November 7. Because Missouri shared its northern border with Iowa—and the battle of Lexington, Missouri, was but one hundred miles away—Gov. Samuel Kirkwood of Iowa rapidly encouraged the enlistment and participation of every able-bodied man in the state.

Reports from the war began to fill the pages of the *Weekly Ledger* in Fairfield, about five miles southeast of Brookville. On October 21, 1861, the paper told of the Rebels confiscating northerner-owned property in Virginia valued at $800,000 and consisting of "negroes, cotton, sugar, rice, articles there on sale, machinery, ships &c." The story warned that the Confederates would continue to take property to finance their war effort, and that the total of northern investments in the "disloyal states" was estimated at "$250 million, equal to half the debt the U.S. Government is authorized to incur in quelling the rebellion."

If that wasn't frightening enough, an accompanying article in the paper chastised Jefferson County residents for not being adequately supportive at this early stage in the war.

"We are much afraid that Jefferson County will only have credit for sending two companies to fight the battles of our country," the story began. One company of infantry and one of cavalry had been sent, but neighboring Keokuk County, with a much smaller population, already had sent four, the article pointed out.

"Other counties are bragging and boasting of the number of companies which they have sent off," the writer scolded, adding that some Jefferson County men had enlisted in other counties.

With a barrage of scary war news and editorial statements encouraging countywide enlistment in every edition, Jefferson County men such as Gantz must have begun the soul-searching process with increased regularity.

Gantz's father, John, had supported the Democratic party until 1856 when he voted for abolitionist John Fremont for president and remained a Republican thereafter.[2] Gantz, too, was a Republican and later would be called a "stalwart advocate of party principles."[3]

Late in the fall, his mind was made up, and on November 25, 1861—just three days before his twenty-sixth birthday—Gantz left Louisa and Byron to volunteer in the Fourth Iowa Cavalry at Mount Pleasant, Iowa. He wasn't the only family member who left the crop fields for the battle fields. Three brothers and two brothers-in-law each decided to serve in the Civil War—all of them either in the Third or Fourth Iowa cavalries.

Brother Andrew enlisted on August 26, 1861, in the Third; brother William enlisted November 1, 1861, in the Third; Joseph Ennis, husband of sister Maria, enlisted November 2, 1861, in the Fourth; E.G. Dearduff, husband of sister Martha, enlisted November 12, 1861, in the Fourth; and youngest brother John T., who was only eighteen years old when the war broke out, enlisted on February 11, 1864, in the

Louisa S. Gantz and Byron Noble Gantz,
wife and son of Jacob S. Gantz.

Andrew Gantz,
brother of Jacob S. Gantz.

Third.

Shortly after Gantz enlisted, a reporter from the Fairfield *Ledger* visited the Fourth Iowa Cavalry and wrote of conditions in camp:

On Thursday, we visited the 4th regiment of the Iowa Cavalry, rendezvoused at Mount Pleasant under command of Col. Porter, who so gallantly distinguished himself at the battle of Wilson's Creek (Missouri, Aug. 10, 1861) while Major of the 1st regiment Infantry. The regiment is located about one mile west of Mt. Pleasant, on a beautiful piece of ground, where frame buildings have been erected, affording excellent accommodations for the troops. We found them enjoying themselves as well as could be expected under the circumstances. The boys are well satisfied with their connection with Uncle Sam thus far. They were expecting to be sworn into the U.S. service the day we were there, but were disappointed. On Saturday following, however, Capt. Chambers, of the regular army, arrived, and swore four companies into service. Several of the Captains were not sworn in, as their companies were not full. Among those was Capt. Pierce, who required three men to fill his company. He was here on Tuesday hunting for that number and we presume he got them. They expect to get their clothing in two or three weeks. At present, there is some suffering among the troops on account of an insufficient supply of blankets and quilts. We are asked to state, for the knowledge of our patriotic citizens, that those who [have] blankets or quilts to spare will find them very welcomely received at 'Camp Harlan.' If our citizens desire their blankets and quilts returned, they can place a mark on them and when the government blankets are received at 'Camp Harlan' those sent from here can be returned. We trust an effort will be made to at least furnish Capt. Pierce's company with sufficient bed clothing. The purchase of horses for the regiment has not yet commenced; we understand, however, that $120,000 has been placed to the account of Col. Porter's regiment for the purchase of horses.

The Fourth Iowa Cavalry, one of nine cavalry units formed in Iowa, had been authorized by President Lincoln in a July 23, 1861, proclamation. The twelve original companies—A, B, C, D, E, F, G, H, I, K, L, and M—began in August filling the newly built barracks in Camp Harlan, which was named in honor of the state senator who lived in that town. By January 1, 1862, the Fourth Iowa Cavalry had 1,086 men and officers ready for war.[4]

With an excellent herd of horses, but a poor supply of weapons, the regiment at the end of February 1862 left Camp Harlan on a train to St. Louis, Missouri, and Benton Barracks where they stayed for several weeks acting primarily as guards and escorts for supplies to other troops in the southwest. In March, the regiment gathered in Springfield, Missouri. By mid-April, the regiment had moved to Forsyth, Missouri, near the Arkansas border and then to West Plains, Missouri. In the two months they had been gone from Iowa, the Fourth Iowa Cavalry had only lost one man—Lt. William Heacock of Company F—in a battle at Talbot's Ferry, Arkansas. But many of the men had died or been discharged as unable to serve because of disease.[5]

The problems with illness might have been attributed to the stress and hardships of travel, to the fact that so many men came from isolated rural areas and had not been exposed to diseases before, or to the fact that this period preceded the era of medical discoveries linking illness to sanitation. But another cause identified in an investigation of 1861 enlistment procedures in the North, "estimated that 25 percent of the recruits should have been rejected for medical reasons."[6]

Despite the toll sickness took on the troops, the Fourth Iowa Cavalry moved to Batesville, Arkansas, and then to Helena, Arkansas, arriving July 12, 1862, where they would settle for about eight months. Travel to Helena was extremely slow mainly because of the extreme heat of the summer in the South, the large number of sick soldiers, the enemy-blocked roads, and the need for constant foraging for the horses.[7]

Helena was an important post and had been threatened with attack by the Rebels many times. In their eight months there, the Fourth Iowa Cavalry scouted and guarded the place where also stationed were four regiments—three infantry and one battery. Camp was about four miles outside of town on the Little Rock Road in a key position that would make it the first to encounter an approaching Rebel force. Therefore, the Fourth Iowa Cavalry had to maintain a constant watch for the Confederate army by sending scouts in the advance of heavy picket lines.[8]

From September 1862 until March 1863, when Gantz's diaries begin, the Fourth Iowa Cavalry was involved in about four fights, which resulted in a relatively small number of men killed, wounded, or taken prisoner. Most of the prisoners were exchanged within a couple of months of their capture.

It was during this time, when the regiment went on a week-long march through Friars' Point and Grenada, Mississippi, that several hundred black men joined the army. Allowing black men to become Union soldiers was prohibited until Congress passed the controversial authorizing legislation in July 1862. Curiously, though the Union was fighting an abolitionist's war, there still was a negative racial attitude among many of the northern troops. Gantz mentioned on three occasions having about fifty black men in his regiment. He called them "darkies," although not in a hateful tone, as he mentioned that the "darkies are coocking everything we will give them," that they "had a dance last night," and that they had a meeting "in our church . . . formed a class and several of them joined."

When the regiment returned in December 1862 to Helena, Arkansas, it was again plagued with illnesses apparently caused by poor conditions in the damp camp near the Mississippi River.[9] Indeed, Gantz's writing began on March 12, 1863, and within a few days he mentioned being very sick with a cold.

Among the infectious diseases most prevalent in the Union army between 1861 and 1866 were: (1) diarrhea, dysentery, and cholera with about 1.8 million cases reported and 44,863 deaths; (2) malaria with 1.3 million cases and 10,063 deaths; (3) catarrh and bronchitis with 283,075 cases and 585 deaths; (4) typhoid fever with 148,631 cases and 34,833 deaths; (5) gonorrhea with 102,893 cases and 7 deaths; (6) ophthalmia and conjunctiva with 84,986 cases and 4 deaths; (7) boils with 83,170 cases and no deaths; (8) syphilis with 79,589 cases and 151 deaths; (9) pneumonia with 77,335 cases and 19,971 deaths; and (10) jaundice with 77,236 cases and 414 deaths.[10]

There also were about half a million cases of tonsillitis, mumps, abscesses, tuberculosis, smallpox, inflammation of the liver, diphtheria, inflammation of the brain, meninges, and spinal cord, various fevers, and other diseases that caused almost 30,000 deaths. Several thousand deaths also were attributed to noninfectious diseases such as sunstroke, scurvy, and rheumatism. Many of those who contracted these conditions did not die but were discharged as unable to continue in the service.[11]

In his two years of journalizing, Gantz mentioned his health or that of his comrades in thirteen of the months. Gantz often had colds, but he also had diarrhea, according to medical records obtained from the National Archives, and he was treated for ophthalmia and a boil. Though he had three of the top ten infectious diseases, Gantz apparently was a brawny farmer of German extraction who, his military records state, stood 5'11" and weighed slightly more than 180 pounds. He effectively conquered his illnesses and on many of the days when he was not sick, Gantz spent time sitting with his ill buddies in the hospital.

Mrs. M. E. Woods of Fairfield, who volunteered as a nurse and was appointed a sanitary agent February 11, 1863, visited the Fourth

Iowa Cavalry in October of that year, Gantz noted. The Sanitary Commission was a volunteer agency funded and staffed by private citizens. From its beginning on September 5, 1861, until the end of the war, the Western Sanitary Commission provided more than 4.2 million articles valued at $3.5 million.[12] These items, which ranged from bedding, clothing, medical supplies, and books to stationery, games, and liquor, were meant to supplement what the government could provide.

Occasional reference to sanitary provisions was made by Gantz. In March 1863, he mentioned that Company M got "cakes, apels, potatoes, onions, butter" and many other things too numerous for him to list. His company once was disappointed when they returned to camp after an eighteen-day scout to find a supply of sanitary goods all spoiled.

As Gantz was a company cook who spent much of his time from August 1863 until March 1864 baking pies and bread, his comments often referred to the status of the food supply. Typically, the company drew rations for five- to ten-day periods, but there were several instances when they went without. This was not a crisis if they happened to be near a fertile plantation during the growing season. Gantz seemed almost to drool as he talked of foraging the countryside for hogs, chickens, and fresh fruits and vegetables.

In fact, the troops became so accustomed to having the plantations' plentiful produce that Gantz bemoaned one morning in Alabama in 1865 having for breakfast only "hardtack and coffey"—the usual government ration. He also improvised at one point on the prairie when the company had gone without rations having nothing but beef to eat for about four days. Gantz boiled and gritted corn intended for the horses and made corn cakes for the men.

Gantz and his fellow cavalrymen spent about as much time scouting for horse feed as they did for the enemy. Like the men, the horses occasionally had to go without feed for an extended period until either a shipment of corn came in on a train or a supply was found growing on a farm through which the regiment was passing. The horse herd required a lot of work, and Gantz reported practically every month having to tend to the needs of the animals—having them shod, having no place to tie them on the prairie, having to trade them in, and having to guard them at night.

Through all of this—the battle fatigue, witnessing death and destruction, being ill and without proper care and provisions—it was inevitable that sadness from time to time would slip into camp. But

Gantz didn't dwell on despair.

He never voiced any opposition to the Union cause or disgust with each turn of the calendar's pages over three and a half years of wearisome service on the battlegrounds. He did, from time to time, talk of being homesick on one hand but on the other, "so tiered and dirty I could hardely read" letters from his wife. Beyond that, Gantz's sporadic sources of sorrow stemmed from poor camping conditions, not receiving mail, and the health of his regiment and the horse herd. He also mentioned not being able to vote in the presidential election of 1864—a situation that must have bothered this civic-minded Iowan.

When those situations improved, however, Gantz was generous with his pleasantries. He often wrote that "it is a fine day." The troops had a swing during their long stay in Helena, Arkansas, swam in a cistern at a cotton gin near one camp, and celebrated the surrender of Vicksburg, Mississippi, by making lemonade and taking the rest of the day off on July 4, 1863. Good times also were had with friends in camp or with old acquaintances from Iowa when their paths crossed.

As a farmer, Gantz scrutinized the countryside on the long journeys through plantations, orchards, mountainous areas, pine forests, large prairies, rivers, and streams. This northerner saw for the first time magnolia trees, an alligator, and large "nats" hovering over the swamps.

Perhaps his greatest source of pleasure was receiving mail from home or attending "preaching" meets in camp. Although he didn't always record the postmark date on his wife's letters, his few references to that fact indicated that Louisa normally mailed a letter to Gantz every Monday. Those letters, however, reached the soldier in varying lengths of time from eight to twenty days after she mailed them. There was a two-month period from August 22 to October 23, 1863, in which Gantz didn't list receiving any letters while stationed in the vicinity of Vicksburg. He continued to write regularly to Louisa and other relatives and mentioned that it was disappointing not to receive a reply.

Gantz regularly attended preaching by the company chaplain during 1863 and 1864. He didn't mention whether the church services leaned toward a particular persuasion. He had been raised in a Baptist family but, at least after the war, was a devout Methodist.[13]

There was a new church built for the troops, Gantz reported, in February 1864—the place where the black soldiers formed a separate group and joined the church. He also attended a sermon while on board the *U.S. Constitution* heading home on furlough. And while stationed at Benton Barracks in St. Louis, Gantz went to the Christian Commission—a charitable entity, which provided Union soldiers with recreational alternatives to the doldrums of camp life. The church aptly was there at the end when Gantz was critically wounded while guarding a Rebel commissary near the railroad. It was to a church five miles south of Plantersville, Alabama, that Gantz and four other wounded were taken to wait for transport to a hospital.

In the diaries that follow, Gantz's words will take the reader across thousands of miles of the central and southern United States as the dark eyes of this Iowa farmer are opened to the charm of the country and the wretchedness of war.

II

The Diaries

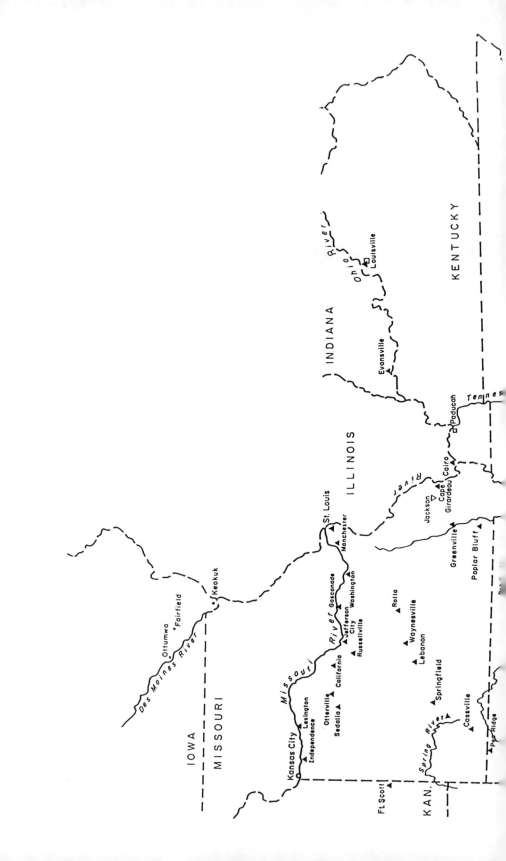

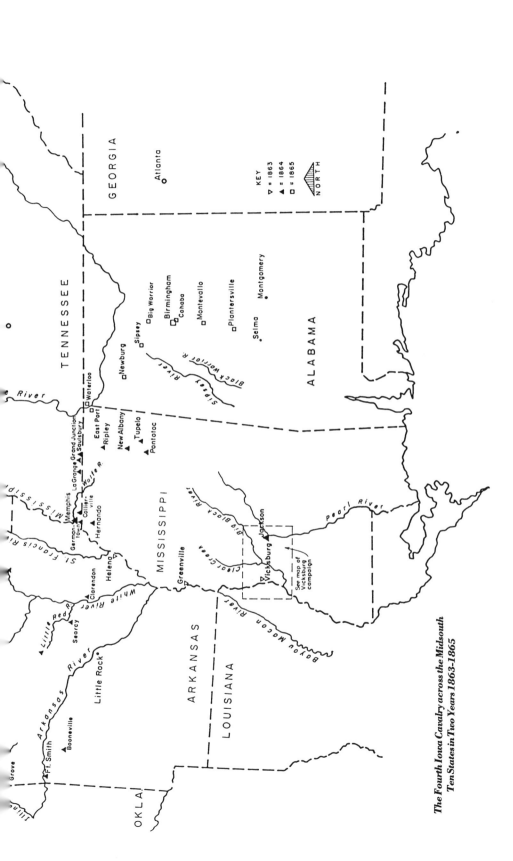

The Fourth Iowa Cavalry across the Midsouth
Ten States in Two Years 1863-1865

KEY

∇ = 1863
▲ = 1864
□ = 1865

NORTH

GEORGIA

Atlanta

TENNESSEE

Big Warrior
Birmingham
Cahaba
Montevallo
Sipsey
Plantersville
Newburg
Selma
Montgomery

Waterloo

ALABAMA

East Port
Ripley
New Albany
Tupelo
Pontotoc

Grand Junction
Saulsbury
La Grange
Memphis
Collier-
ville
Germantown
Hernando

Wolf R.

River

MISSISSIPPI

St. Francis River

Helena

Clarendon

White River

Searcy

Greenville

Big Black River

Clear Creek

Jackson
Pearl River

Vicksburg

See map of
Vicksburg
campaign

Little Red R.

Little Rock

Arkansas River

Booneville

Ft. Smith

Bayou Macon River

Red R.

ARKANSAS

LOUISIANA

OKLA.

Grove

Sipsey River
Black Warrior R.

NORTH

SATARTIA
6/4/5
MECHANICSBURG
5/29

? ROACH'S
5/23-25
6/1, 7, 9

(HAYNE'S
BLUFF)

YAZOO RIVER

5/28, 31
6/2
6/12
7/5
6/18
6/27
5/17

VICKSBURG
5/19, 22

BROWNSVILLE
5/18

7/7
7/8
5/16

7/6

5/26

JACKSON
(7/15+)
7/14

RAYMOND
5/13

CAYUGA
5/10

Big Black River

GRAND GULF

MISSISSIPPI RIVER

4/30
5/7
5/8
5/4

KEY

- - - - Probable route
· · · · · Conjectured route
⌂ Camp
⌂? Conjectured camp
★ Skirmish or battle
5/30 Date of event

0   3   6
miles

The Vicksburg Campaign

Jacob S. Gantz and the Vicksburg Campaign

by JAMES W. WHITAKER

apping a portion of the movements of Jacob Gantz during April through July of 1863 illustrates some realities of warfare in general and the Vicksburg campaign in particular. The diary itself documents the ability of the troops to keep in touch with the home front, as the army was able to deliver mail in a fairly regular way to Gantz's cavalry unit. The map shows the river and bayou system, which had frustrated attempts to attack Vicksburg from the north and west. A second observation from the map is that although Gantz's unit was in enemy territory and moved around frequently, it had remarkably little direct contact with the enemy. Here at one of the crucial battles of the war, from the perspective of Gantz, there was much ado but no real participation in the great event. That, of course, was better than being wounded or killed in direct action, but it does document a reality of war. For every direct battle, there is a lot of support and reconnaissance effort. The number of troops available to be used may be as important as the number in the battle line.

In the Vicksburg campaign, in particular, Gantz's unit and others were performing the very necessary function of keeping tabs on, and preparing to attack, Confederate forces to the east that might threaten the Union troops besieging Vicksburg. The success of the campaign depended upon keeping the two major Confederate armies under Generals Pemberton (at Vicksburg) and Johnston (east and

---

James W. Whitaker is an associate professor of history at Iowa State University, Ames.

north of Jackson) from uniting to threaten the Union forces under General Grant.

For Gantz, the Vicksburg campaign began on April 29 when his unit left Helena, Arkansas, for Milliken's Bend on the west side of the Mississippi above Vicksburg. Grant, having tried several times to get at the city from the north on the east side of the Mississippi (or with a combined land and river attack), decided in April 1863 to pass below the city on the west side, cross the river, and come at Vicksburg from the south and east. It was a daring strategy that involved keeping the two Confederate armies apart so that he would not have to face the combined force all at once. Gantz and his unit were not in the vanguard (the first Union troops crossed to the east side of the river below Grand Gulf on April 30) but supported the battle plan Grant quickly developed—cut loose from his base, get between the two Confederate armies, attack Jackson (which forced Johnston's forces to retreat to the northeast on May 14), and turn back toward Vicksburg. Pemberton decided on the fourteenth to move southeast from Vicksburg to cut Grant's supply line (which did not exist) thus giving Grant time to get firmly between the two Confederate forces. Pemberton retreated into Vicksburg, thus trapping his army. On the nineteenth, Union troops took possession of Hayne's Bluff north of Vicksburg and reopened communications with the Mississippi base. That same day a direct attack on Vicksburg failed and a siege began, which ended on July 4. Gantz's unit, often just a day behind the main action, assisted in the clearing of Jackson and occupation of Hayne's Bluff but mostly scouted on the northeast rear of the siege troops.

The map shows movements of Gantz's unit from April 30 to just after the surrender of Vicksburg. Some of the movement is adequately documented, some is inferred from the diary entries when compared to contemporary maps. The diary entries indicate when the unit remained in camp. (The base map was adapted from Vincent J. Esposito, ed., *The West Point Atlas of American Wars* [New York: Praeger, 1959], v. 1, map 104.)

1863

THIS first diary was written in a slender, palm-size daily register that has no cover.

This book belongs to Jacob S. Gantz, private, of Co. M, fourth regimen of iowa, volunteer cavalry. residence when at home Brookville, Jefferson County Iowa. was born in Ohio in the year 1835 on the 28th day of November. was married in the year 1858 on the first day of December & enlisted in the armey of the USA in the year 1862 [his mistake, it actually was 1861] on the 25 day of November.

Any one finding this book will do the owner a great favor to hand it to him & if he gets killed, some friend will please send this & the rest of my things to my friends at Brookville, Jefferson Iowa to Mrs. Louisa S. Gantz,* wife of Jacob S. Gantz. Aprile 6, A.D. 1863 date of riting.

diary and memorandum book for 1863. owner Jacob S. Gantz. bought from John M. Kelley [Kelly].*

The spelling and grammar in this transcription of the diaries are retained as Jacob Gantz wrote. People and significant dates, noted by an asterisk (*), are identified in the appendix.

March 1863

HELENA, ARKANSAS

The 4th Iowa Cavalry moved toward Helena, Arkansas, on June 24, 1862. The Union army had captured Memphis, Tennessee, little more than two weeks earlier and Helena was mere miles south on the Mississippi River. Helena was considered an important post and had been threatened by attack many times. The Fourth Iowa Cavalry reached Helena on July 12, 1862. Gen. U. S. Grant was headquartered at Memphis since its capture and, by the time Gantz's diary opens, was masterminding an attack on Vicksburg, Mississippi, which already had staved off the Union forces in an earlier attack.

12: we have been laying idle all day. we have plenty of much fun here & the boys have ben eating all day. their is allso a kind of tree here that is very huge & has very huge white flowers on it. is called the magnolia tree

13: today eli [Dearduff]* and Jos. [Ennis]* & myself went to town to get our potographs taken but could not get them. then we got a very good dinner & came home. I got my degarotype taken today.

14: sateurday. nothing of importence only it was a very nice day

15: we was inspected by major parkell in the fore noon & in the afternoon the quarters was inspected by all the staff. they allso got a ride on our swing

16: today I went to town with some refund horses to turn over. this regiment sent 82 horses that was broke down & not fit for the service.

17: this was a very beautiful day. i was on duty piling up oats. about noon I got a letter from lou & it mailed the 9th. I also rote a letter to lou & put $6 in it & one to father with 20 dol. sent my likenes in lous.

18: this is a very beautiful day. the first thing we done was a dismounted skirmish. the next was to shoot at targets 3 rounds a peace. Wm. Lee* & me washed ourselves & cloths. it was very hot weather

19: this is a very nice day. nothing of importence only their was a detail for a scout

20: this morning at 3 oc they started. I did not go for I could get no horse fit. the day was very warm & cloudy. I was on stable gard to night

21: today was very pleasant but rather warm. James Bell [Beall]* started home

22: today was cloudy & raned a little. I rote to cousin beca today & allso rote on for craff*

23: this was rather a cloudy day. the scout came in this eavening. I did not do very much. one night they lost 40 horses. the nats killed them. some of the men came in dismount & some found horses.

24: this day was very pleasant. I was on gard last night. male came today. I got a letter from lou. heard that andrew [Gantz]* was home. I allso rote a letter to lou today in answer

25: nothing of importence today only we drew 6 days ration

26: today their was 20 men detailed out of each co. to poleace the quarters. I was one. I also got a letter from lou with her likeness in. willcox [Wilcox]* paid me one dollar & a half

27: today nothing of importence. we heard that the 18th iowa was at helena so I went down but they did not come. Tom McMurey [McMurray]* shot himself through the hand axcidently while fishing

28: nothing of importence today

29: I was on picket today & it stormed, blowed & snowed all night & day which made it very disagreeable. their was allso a scout out today but they did not do very much.

30: this morning came in off of picket. it was still cold & storming. today the 4th Iowa. Cav. drew 150 horses. Co. M got 21 horses. their was allso a lot of sanitary goods came for Co. M such as cakes, apels, potatoes, onions, butter and many other things to to to men.

31: No. 4 rec. this morning they sent a lot of old horses. I allso drew 10 days rations. their was allso a large mail came in. I got a letter from Louisa. I allso answer it. I had a bad cold. I was very sick. put 10 cnts in [the letter]

April 1863

1: today was a very fine day. nothing of importence ocurred until about 3 oclock that night. their was about 50 gorillas sliped up on our pickets, fiered in to them, wounded. wounded 4 of the kansas 5th prety bad. their lieut. run to camp & left them. our lieut. went to them as much as he could

2: today nothing of importence only a smaller unit went out & found 3 of the secesh. wounded one lieuten severely. I was on fateague & was very sick. kept my bed in the afternoon

3: today was a very fine day. nothing of importence occurred. I was better today

4*: weather was a little windy. one man died this morning in the hospital from the 25th Iowa. I am still better today but not able for duty

5: rowes [Rowe]* wife came. weather very nice. had inspection at 8 oclock. a scout started out at 3 oc. each men from Co. M to be gone for 5 days. had preaching at 10 from Kirkpatrick.* feel prety well today but have been thinking about home

6: very warm & pleasant, a little windy. 10 new sadles drawed for Co. M. nothing new in camp. this eavening I feel pretty well

7: date of letters to lous No. 1 rec. this was a very beautiful day. the first thing I done was to wash some cloths. after that the mail came in & I got a letter from louisa s. Gantz. I then set down & rote one to lou in answer. after dark we heard some holowing at head quarters. i went over. we had some good speaking

8: this was a very fine morning. I was on fateague duty moving Co. L quarters. in the afternoon Co. M drawed 8 more horses. towards eavening it clouded up and had the afearing of rain

9: but this morning was clear again & very warm. their is nothing of importence today

10: today I was on gard. the scout came about 3 oc in the afternoon. brought in some very good news & some very bad news [blurred] into a squad of [blurred] killed one Co. L man & wounded 4, but we fired & wounded a great many [blurred]

11: This morning I came off of gard & felt fine. we had general muster today. we allso signed the pay roll this eavening & we had a very nice rain & we neaded it for it was very dry

12: this was one just as nice mornings as I ever saw. everything looked green & nice. I felt just like I would like to be at home. Our chaplain preached & I liked his searmon. Josef [Ennis]* & me got our likeness taken.

13: this was a very nice morning. nothing of importence occurred. in the afternoon it clouded up & began to rain. in the eavening it raned all night. I rote a letter for Craff [Craft].*

[Entries for 14–19 are missing.]

20: i was on picket today. the weather was very fine but the mesketo was so bad they nearly eat us up. we did not see any enemy out but heard five shots on the other posts through the night

21: letter No. 3. this morning came off of picket. it was a little cloudy. I got weighed & weighed 182 lbs. the mail came in & I got no letter. this afternoon we got our pay. we got 52 dollars. I sent a letter to lou with 20 cts in it.

22: today we moved our stables. we allso had regimental drill. while we was drilling their was a horse race cloce to the drill ground

23: I rote a letter for how [Howe]* 20 dollars in it. this morning their was a scout went from this regiment of 200 men. I was on the detail but another fellow wanted me to stand gard in his place & him go so I am on gard today. I got a letter from louisa today. I was to meeting tonight. this was a fine day

24: this morning before I came off of gard we had a very hard rain. this afternoon we done up our overcoats to send home. I rote a letter for Craff [Craft]* & allso one for how [Howe]* & put 2 dollars in. I allso rote a letter to father & put 20 dollars in. we got orders to move today

25: letter No. 4. today nothing of importence onley we was prepareing to march. I allso rote a letter to lou. last night we had speaking. I allso sent 25 dollars in lous letter

26: this morning was cloudy. we had nothing of importence today onley preaching. this afternoon it rained. today their was some infantry came out to hold our picket post

27: today I was on picket & it rained very hard & we went to a house & their was 3 or 4 widows their & their was some of the soldiers came out & hugged them then [blur] and myself & another fellow wached them

28: this morning came in off of picket & it was clear. about an hour after we came off of gard we got orders to march. the orders was countermanded so we did not go that day

Grant's plan to move a force of forty thousand men to take Vicksburg, Mississippi, begins. The Union army had captured control of Memphis, Tennessee, and New Orleans, Louisiana, so Vicksburg remained as the last major port on the Mississippi River that would give the Union complete control and enable it to slash the Confederate transport of supplies. Confederate General Pemberton rallied some twenty thousand soldiers, scattered in various positions in the region, in defense of the river city.

29: letter no. 5. I rote a letter to louisa this morning rite away. after breckfast we got orders to go to town immediate so we went & was all day getting on the boats. about 6 oclock the 4 iowa left helena & a great many of them was so tite they could hardly walk

30: we are now in luisina. well this morning when I woked we was below the mouth of white river. about 9 oclock we past greenville, a lonely deserted place. we came on untill about 3 oc when we landed at millikens bend. some of the 30 boys came to see us

May 1863

1: this morning at 6 oc we started on a 3 day scout. we foled around until noon then we got a start & went through some of the pretiest country I ever saw. the buffalow nats was so bad we could hardly go. we went about 20 miles up the river & camped

2: last night we camped at davises landing on a very nice farm. today we went on to the age of byo [bayou] macon in about 6 miles of where their was said to [be] 15 hundred secesh but we could go no further for the swamp. then we fed & started back & came in 2 miles of where we camped last night

3: this is a very nice morning. about 8 oc we started for camp rite through a swamp part of the country where the nats was so bad we could hardely see. we got to camp about noon. I rote to louisa

4: letter no. 6. this was a very nice morning. I started on a march today at 10 oc. it was very hot. about 3 in the afternoon we came to a little town the name of richmond where their was 2 regiments. then we came about 4 miles & camped in very nice place

5: I was on gard last night. last night it rained. this morning we started about 7. about 10 oc we met 450 secesh prisoners that was taken at grand gulf. about 1 oc we camped near a division of inf. camp. at this place I saw an aligator. they sent one down to cartherige to report the regiment present & to get the orders

6: last night it was very cool. we did not get marching orders untill about noon. then we started & marched about 6 miles & then camped for the night. this eavening their was 140 more secesh prisoners went through. very cool all day

7: this was a very nice morning. we start at 7 oc for G. Gulf, Co. M rear. we eat diner on perkins plantation J.D. [blur]. tonight we camped on ruths plantation on Lake St. Joseph where their was the greatest distrtion of prorerty I ever saw. here lived a set of J.Ds relations some [blur] 200,000

8: letter No. 7. we left ruths plantation this morning & got to the river at Grand gulf about 9 oc & their we layed untill night. then we got on boats to come down the river about 4 miles & landed on the Miss. side. we got here about 11 oc at night. was tired & sleepy but the wagons is back

9: this morning when we wakened we found ourselves in a very rough country [went] about 2 miles & fed & are now wating for the teams. the teams did not come untill after dark so we did not leave but we got orders to march at 2

10: very warm & dusty. this morning we marched at 4 & about 10 oc we came where the 30 iowa was. stoped about 3 hours. then we marched about 8 miles & fed & eat on a very nice plantation where we got plenty to eat. that man had about 15 bbls of molasses, 2 bbl of peach brandy & plenty of meat. then we marched about 8 to cayuga & camped

11: hot today. this morning about [blur] oc we got marching orders. we [blur] went in the advance of grants armey. we are now in the advance. it is a little more dangerous but we get plenty to eat of everything. we was in the adv our reg

12: letter no. 8. I started a letter to lou. this morning we are at a very nice place. this morning at 8 we marched. about 11 we run into the rebels. 4 iowa was in advance. we had some heavy firing for a while. got several men killed. we are fixing a bridge now. we march—heavy fiering—5 miles a heat at raymond

13: very hot. this morning at 2 we had rev. we marched, Co. M in advance. about 10 we got to raymond. there our right flank had a fight yesterday. both sides lost a great many but we whipped them bad. about 2 oc we took the advance of the armey. Co. M saw about 30 secesh & got 3 pris. camped at the Miss Springs. we saw lots of rebs they did [blur]

14: very hot. this morning we advanced but they was gone. we got 3 deserters. about 10 Co. M made a front move. chaced a lot of secesh away from their breckfast & eat it ourselves. about 2 oc we run into some rebels near jackson. had a fight. got them to retreating. run them in & out of jack. they skedadeled & left everything. it was raining all day & we was tierd

15: well after we—pleasant—got supper which was after night we was ordered to sadel so we sadeled & rod all night through the mud & in the secesh lines. today at 2 we got back. we have road 2 days & one night without sleeping any. we saw plenty of secesh at brandon but we onley had 200 men

16: warm & pleasant. this morning we left jackson. about left the town on fire we had a hard time getting the drunk men out. a great many was left because they was drunk. they could not walk well. we stayed at the clinton & fed then marched all night. overtake another division that was [blur] at the R. bridge

17: very warm. this morning we went to the hospitals where they had their wounded & their was a great many. we had a very hard batle here at the R. bridge. they got cloce enough to fight club gun twice. I got a letter from lou. we started on a scout

18: very hot. we camped last night 7 miles from the armey. this morning went on about 5 miles further. had a small fight. run into 12 thousand of rebs Johns' men. got 2 boys wounded. past through Brownsville. got plenty of candy then came back crossed black river

19: this morning started before day towards Vicksburg. we

heard some very heavy fireing ever since 9 oc yesterday. when we got in 4 miles of Vick we halted & camped. the 4 Iowa then went out & took Hanes bluff. it had been nearly evacuated. we then came back to camp. all day heavy fireing at Vicksburg

20: warm & nice. we did not have anything to do today only escort the train after corn for the horses & eat strawburie, plumbs & mullburies. we are laying in 4 miles of vicksburg. their has been very heavy fireing ever since the 18th

21: letter No. 9th rec. this morning we moved our camp one mile nearer town. very heavy heavy fireing. between 5 & 7 musketry seased. Co. M detailed a picket. we had some rain. did not fight very hard today. received a letter from lou

22: after we cam in, we rested. our forces began to charge on vicksburg about 1 oc & such fighting I never want to be near again while I live. the hard fireing seased about 8 oc but some fireing continued all night. our forces gained some on them all day & are now holding a pretty good posision

23: cloudy. this morning they began very early to fight at vicksburg but seased about 2 oc and did not fire any till 12 oc. then we left on a scout. went a past Hanes bluff & camped 4 miles beyond on roaches plantation where they had plenty. very hot & dry

24: very beautiful morning. we left for Yazoo City by the way of mechanicksville. when we got within 6 miles of town we run on to their pickets. got 6 prisoners. chaced them 3 miles. run on to a large force of infantry & artillery & had to retreat with [blur] of one man killed & 2 wounded

25: warm but pleasant. we had to come back to where we camped last night which made a ride of 60 miles which kept us till near this morning—where we are now resting & the darkies are coocking everything we will give them & they have about 50 camped here & we got some milk today. well we camped at roaches last night again

26: received a letter from lou & etie. this morning we left roaches. started toward vicksburg but when we got to Hanes bluff we started for black river Rail R. bridge where we camped near. going to start from their in the morning on another scout but i do not no where to

27: letter 10th rec. very hot. this morning we left black river railroad bridge & went nearly back to Hanes bluff & stopped at a plantation to feed. while we was their one division of infantry passed us so then we stayed all night at grants where we fed

28: very pleasant. this morning we started out in advance of the infantry. we had not marched far when we run across some scatering secesh but they skedadaled. we camped at a plantation where the man had been prety well asset but had run away. his name was bart cah in secesh armey

29: very hot rained some about noon. we left Hanes this morning about 6 oc & about 10 oc we got to mechanicsbg where we had a very hard skirmish & the Cav. 4 io. had to fight them 2 hours before the infantry came up. got 2 men wounded. killed several of them afterward. Co. L got 9 men wounded. we then camped in mechanicsburg

30: last eavening we received orders from grant* to report back to vicksburg so this morning we started but we onley marched about 10 miles untill we camped on a very nice farm. it rained this afternon

31: very pleasant in the morning. this morning had a smal skirmish got one man wounded. towards eavening was fiered into agan but no damage. we camped at hanes bluff to night. through the day was very hot. we are all about woried and tired out for the want of rest

June 1863

1: very dry and hot. this morning enstead of going to camp we was ordered out on a scout but we did not go far untill we got around to old roaches plantation where our regiment stoped to camp. we then put 2 companies out on picket

2: letter no. 11th rec. last night our pickets was fiered into once but done no harm. today we was reinforced with the 5 illinois. I rote a letter to louisa s. gantz. 4th iowa received 130 union guns today

3: letter no. 12 rec warm but pleasant. we are at roaches yet. it is cloudy and pleasant. I got a letter from louisa with 7 postage stamps in. I allso answered it & etties. this eavening at 6 oc we started on a scout & marched about 15 miles before we camped. we have a whole brigade of Cav.

4: camped at mierses plantation. this morning we started early. about 5 oc skirmishing began. then we sent a regimen on each road & had some fighting on every road. then half of our regiment started for the boats. we saw 200 ses [secesh] but they run when we got to them. the infantry was fighting but then we whiped them. we are now at satarshia

5: last night we camped at satarshia. Co. was on picket—very hot & dry—this morning we came to mechanicsville where we had a hard fight yesterday & whiped the rebell & burnt the town. they run a canon close to our boats & fiered on them but our gunboats made them skedadel. this eavening we moved back between mechanicsburg & satarshia & camped.

6: very hot. this morning we was ordered on a scout & we started then. then the order was countermanded so we came back & camped. about 10 we got orders to march back to Hanes bluff. about 12 we started & it was so hot that 7 of the infantry was sun struck & 2 fell dead. 1 cap shot himself accidentally & died. we only marched about 10 miles today.

7: this morning the infantry started at 5 oc, cav at 6 oc. got to roaches about 7 oc. the gorilla was shooting at the rear all day. when we got here their was about 200 men that was gave out so that they could go no farther. i was nearly over come with heat for it was very hot & dry

8: this was a very warm day but we did not have any thing to do so we got to rest for the first time in 5 weeks. we was camped at a large coton gin where there was a very large cisteren to swim in. I got a letter from lou

9: we are at raches & getting reinforcement all the time. about noon we got orders to march in 2 hours so we got ready but did not know we was going when we started. we went to camp for the first time for 18 days. when we got their we found some sanitary goods nearly all spoiled

10: rained hard all day. this morning it was raining. we was ordered out on a scout but I did not go for I was about tiered out & got permission to rest for one day. this eavening the scout returned but saw no rebels

11: letter rec. no. 13th. very pleasant. this morning we went out on a one day scout to blockade roads. we was out all day but saw no secesh. when we came back the camp was moved & their was a letter in camp for me from lou

12: this was a very pleasant day. nothing of importence in camp today. we are now resting at milldale camp. they are not doing much as vicksburg

13: this morning very pleasant. Co. M was on a picket. we had a very pleasant day of it & did not see any rebels. our camp moved to day. we was expecting an attact on our road

14: awful hot. this was a very pleasant day. we did not see any rebs last night but this the infantry pickets did not let us in for about 2 hours. we had preaching this eavening by our chaplin. I rote a letter to lou

15: letter no. 14th rec. this morning Co. M & B went out on a scout. found some secesh, got 2 horses. their is said to be 15 thou in the advance supposed to be prices [Gen. Sterling Price]* men. some of the troops had a fight on another road. got 20 prisoners. rained very hard this day

16: very pleasant. today our regimen moved. we had orders to report to gen. sherman* for orders. we was then ordered to report to Gen. Osterhouse [Osterhaus].* we then camped in 2 miles of his armey. Co. M went on petroll. got in at 8 oc & it was raining some

17: cloudy but pleasant. we lay in camp untill noon then Co. M & L went on a scout to big black, about 11 miles. did not see any secesh but saw plenty of signs. heard of a force of 15 hinderd reb cavalry & a force of 30 thousand rebs

18: this reg. started out on a 1 day scout. i did not go. the scout went 15 miles, saw some secesh, mad a charge on them & they run. the scout came in at sundown. I went a blackburrying got plenty to eat & stew for the mess

19: this morning Co. M was on picket. I did not go for I was on coocking for squad 5. their was nothing of importence in camp. I got a letter from louisa this eavening dated June 8 No. 15th

20: this morning we heard very heavy canonading at

vicksburg but did not hear the results. I rote a letter to louisa in answer to the one I got yesterday. the health of the regiment is not very good

21: letter No. 15th rec. Company M went out on a scout. got back at noon. 4 or 5 of our boys was very sick. today one of Co. Ls men died today with a congstige chill. some more boys prety bad. the chaplin preached at Co. M quarters at 4 oc

22: warm but pleasant. part of 4 co. 125 men. this morning Co M went out on picket Co A.L.I.K went on a scout. about 10 oc a force of secesh got in their then had to figure how to get out. killed [blur] 9 in all, 6 or 7 mortaley wounded & some—25 missing, 60 horses lost

23: last night our forces ran on their arms. we did not get much sleep. we are reinforced with 10 brigades of infantry & now marching onto the [blur] all the able men were moved out 6 miles. tonight came back 4 miles to the hospital. divisions of infantry went out

24: we lay in camp. did not do very much. a flag of truce came in from the rebels. said they had lost 80 men—missing, killed or wounded. today at 1 oc port hudson was surrendered with [blur]

25: this day across the Port hudson. we moved our camp 4 miles farther on the [blur]. have nothing of importence from the rebels. the sick went to the river. I rote to lou

26: letter No. 16 rec. got a letter from lou. this morning all the men was ordered to the regiment. in the eavening we was ordered in front of the armey for picket. we are expecting an attack here every day. McH shot himself through the face acidently. very warm today

27: very warm & cloudy. we are laying in camp. was mustered to try the strenght of the rebs Co. M mustered 46 men. this afternoon Co. M was outfited to fight. I was on gard at headquarters & was to see reb. we are now camped on bear creek 2 miles from big black & out of rations

28: very hot. camped on bear creek. Co. M on picket. one videt got his finger shot off by a rebel. then the rebel run & we did not cach him but we did not see any more of them. to night drew rations for 2 days. paymaster came

29: cloudy pleasant. some skirmishing in other horse division.

we lay in camp today. nothing of importence here. toward midle of
the day very hot. this eavening the pay master came

30: very hot. letter no. 17th rec. we received 2 months pay &
allso settled for a years clothing. I drew 43.20. I then sent a letter to
lou with a note to father & allso expressed 50 dollars to father

July 1863

1: this was a fine day but very hot. we are still camped on bear
creek where we see some of the secesh every day. some of our boys
are very sick but are getting along very well at presint

2: very hot. Co. M is on picket. their was a scout out from this
regiment. they saw some rebs acrost big black & fiered at them &
came back. eck was here this morning. this eavening cloudy &
looks like rain

3: very hot. this morning our Co returned off of picket. about
noon their was one secesh saw the regiment. went out after them
but they was gone. this eavening we received orders that Vicksburg
was surrendered. clouded up & rained some

4: letter no. 18 to louisa. this morning very quite in camp. the
order was confirmed that Vicksburg was surendered. it was
uncondition. the Col. told us to injouy ourselves so we chered a
while then got some lemons & mad a lot of lemonade. we now have
orders to march towards Jackson tomorow

5: warm & pleasant. we are now geting read to march but we
did not march on the acount of the infantry running across some
rebs at Big Black. they had a prety hard fight their so we are still
laying in the old camp at bear C. our sick all went back

6: very warm we lay here untill noon. our men have been
fighting all day on black. 1 man got killed & 11 wounded. this
afternoon we went down to black & camped. the infantry was
crossing all night on foot [blur] but we could not cross till morning

7: this morning we crossed black then came onto boltons
station where we found large rebels camp. then the cavalry camped
to wate for the infantry. I saw the 30th Iowa. today Co M was on
picket & it rained very hard all night

UPON *the surrender of Vicksburg, Mississippi, General Sherman's army pursued the Rebel forces toward Jackson, Mississippi, which was seized. Part of the railroad tracks was destroyed to further prevent transportation and movement of supplies by the Confederacy. Gantz remained in this general vicinity and was involved in many skirmishes in the area until March 4, 1864, when he and more than five hundred other men were granted a furlough.*

8: very pleasant. we lay in camp untill 3 oc then started towards Jackson. marched 8 miles. found plenty of reb cav. had 2 or 3 skirmish. got 1 man killed, 3 wound. the rebs skedadeled. we then camped for the night

9: very hot. started at 4 without feed. we heard some canonading on another road at 8. then we came to corn & fed them. marched on within 5 miles of Jac. found some more rebs. they got Gen. Osterhos [Osterhaus] * orderly prisiner & shot him. we then stayed all night had considerable skir. all night. rebs skedadeled

10*: cloudy but very warm. we advanced toward jack in force skirmishing all day on all the roads. we are now in cite of Jackson. we then went off to the right flanking but did not see many rebs. we then camped out their. the whole lines are advanceing on Jackson—have a very sore boil under my arm—we have them run in their holes

11: very hot. this morning cav came into the infantry & rested at the deaf & dum crazy assilum. 2 of our boys went amongst the secesh to spy a little. we lay around their till near night then all the cave started out on a scout but I did not go for I had a very sore boil under my arm. they was fighting pretty hard at Jackson. wounded a great many of our men

12: this morning I am with the wagons—very warm—we hear some very heavy fiering at Jackson. our men are ganing on them all day but the rebs are going to stand us a hard fight here. we are very scarce of waughter at this time but have plenty of rosten ears

13: I was with the wagons near Jackson. very heavy fiering at Jackson. the rest of the regiment came in about 3. the mail came through today & I got a letter from louisa date june 29th

14: letter no. 19. very pleasant this morning. we moved camp about 3 miles. we are very scarce of waughter. we lay here in camp the remainder of the day in 5 miles of Jackson north. we are still fighting at Jackson

15: very pleasant. this morning we had orders to move or go on a scout but we did not go. at noon a forage farm went out. we are still camped at the same place. they are still fighting at Jackson

16: warm but pleasant. started at 7 this morning. their was a scout started out of 1 brigade of infantry & one of cav. & one batery. we run across some secesh. part of the cav went to peril river & destroyed the bridge then came about 7 miles & camped for the night on a very nice plantation where we got plenty of corn

17: this morning marched at 5—very pleasant—towards Canton where their is said to be a large force of rebs. when we got within 4 miles of town we run on to them & they was just chargeing on us when we opened on them with our artillery. then they left with some loss. they shot 1 one of our men head off with their artilery—Co. M on picket—& wounded several

18: this morning we went into Canton but the rebs had retreated. the 4th Iowa then went out 8 miles on the B.R. to destroy the bridge and railroad. we then came back 4 miles & fed. while their it rained very hard. we then came back to canton & the troops had all left & all the state buildings was on fire. we then came 3 miles and camped

19: very pleasant morning. at 9 this force started for jackson. we marched 8 miles & fed then marched 5 miles & rested untill the cool of the eavening. then came on to Jackson & camped in the park of the lunatic assilum. their was plenty of crazy in it—men & women

20: very hot at Jackson. this morning we are still in camp at the institute & it is as hot a day as ever I saw. this afternoon we went into Jackson to see the works. we went into peril and baithed then I saw 2 fine union girls & talked with them a while

21: very hot. this morning we started for Vicksburg at 4 oc but we onley marched about 8 miles. then we camped for the night. we are now taking things easy for it is very hot & the infantry can not stand it to march

22: Mt. Heborn. camped at Mt. Heborn institute. this morning we marched about 5 miles, came about 1 mile west of Clinton & camped. sent out a forage train after corn. I went along. we went about 4 miles & found plenty & it was as hot as ever I saw it.

23: Mt. Hebron Cotage. this morning we are still in the same camp. nothing of importence onley this day is not so hot as it was yesterday. we are still at Mount Heborn Cottage. have marching orders in the morning

24: this morning we marched at 7 & marched about 7 miles to boltons station & camped in the sam place we camped when we was going to Jackson. in 2 miles of here their a peach orchard of 30 akers. they are ripe

25: bolton station. warm & pleasant. this morning we are in camp at boltons station. we marched today at noon. came to Big Black & crossed & camped this side. it was after dark when we camped & we was very tierd for it was very hot & dusty

26: got to Bridgeport this morning. we started out to hunt a camp. we got into camp about 11 oc in a very nice grove where we have plenty of waughter. about 1 oc the mail came in & I got a letter from lou dated july 6th No. 20

27: letter No. 20. today we are in camp fixing bunks to rest a while. it rained very hard last night & some today. it is very pleasant now. i saw the 30 iowa today. last night it rained very hard before we got our bunks fixed.

28: Bridgeport. this was a very nice day. nothing of importance going on. we are in camp today poleecing & fixing up our quarters. have a nice camp

29: warm & pleasant. their was a detail of 25 men from Co. M to go to Vicksburg to take some horses. I did not go. it rained very hard this eavening

30: this was a pleasant day. we had to move camp today on the account of ours being too flat but now we are in a better place. I was very sick

31: Bridgeport. very pleasant. we are now in our new camp & pelieceing & fixing up. mail came in this eavening & I got 2 letters from lou No. 21 & 22 dated July 13th and 20th

August 1863

1: lay in camp today. this was a very pleasant day. 3 men started home on furlows from Co. M, D. Thompson*, Wm. Ripley* & R. Young*

2: letter No. 22. this was a very pleasant day. one of our boys died by the name of Jessey Skeears [Skeers].* we also had preaching at 4 oc. I rote a letter for how [Howe] * & allso one to louisa. lieutenant whiting* started home

3: Bridgeport. very warm. nothing of importence. Robert Holland was up to see us. he looks well. their is an order for a scout, ordred out in a few days

4: this was a very hot day. I was down to the 30th to see the boys. John Eller started home today. he was not very well but I think it will cure him to go home

5: nothing of importence. it was very pleasant

6: Bridgeport. warm & pleasant. very hot in the afternoon. I was on gard last night & went out aftr forage today. this eavening clouded up but did not rain

7: very warm. we was nearly all fateague duty, some after corn & some cleaning up the peraide ground. the darkies had a dance in camp last night

8: the train is out after forage. Eli [Dearduff]* went to the 30th Iowa today. William Laughlin* was here this eavening but did not stay only a few minutes

9: letter 29. today we had inspection at 9 oc. we allso drew rations for 5 days. we had preaching at 4 oc. this eavening I rote a letter to lou, letter No. 23

10: Camp near Black river. this morning their was a scout started out to be gone for 20 days. we allso went after forage

11: this day lay in camp. done nothing onley I rote a letter to Beca Patton. 3 men started home on a sick furlow S. Barns [Barnes]*, George Thompson* & Jacob Uptagraft*

12: lay in camp. it was very hot. this eavening I went over to the hospital & set up all night with the sick. their was 2 that was very sick

13: this morning is very warm. I rote a letter to Hows [Howe]*

ORDER NO: 21638
ORDER DATE: 02/14/91

SUCH ARE THE TRIALS : THE CIVIL WAR DIARIES OF
JACOB GANTZ / ED. BY KATHLEEN DAVIS.

IOWA STATE U PR   1991   1 VOLS
                               17.95 CLOTH

0-8138-0947-9 90-48636
N3-629259

                         QTY ORDERED: 001
                         QTY SHIPPED: 001

                              371101/0128

BLACKWELL NORTH AMERICA

FLORIDA STATE UNIV-BACKRUN | 112980023 JUTA-B

wife. we allso drew rations today to last us for 10 days. I allso baked bread

14: very warm. we had nothing of importence going on. this eavening I got a letter from louisa date August 3rd, No. 24, was allso very much pleased with the letter

15: Bridgeport. this is a very hot day. I was on fateague duty today down to the 3rd Iowa. I allso got a letter from lou dated July 27th No. 23

16: letter No. 24th. this morning I went to the 30th Iowa. I got to see the boys. they was all well & harty but the most of them would like to go home. it rained a litle this eavening

17: this morning is very pleasant but I do not feel very well but I guess it is because I do no have enough to do. I feel beter this eavening

18: Bridgeport. this is a very warm day. we are still in the old camp at bridgeport. I feel prety sleapy for I was at the hospital last night siting up with the sick. 1 man was very bad J. Lowman*

19: very pleasant. still laying in camp. the teams went to Vicksburg after forage

20: nothing of importence. still in the same camp

21: letter No. 25th. very pleasant. last night I stayed at the hospit with the sick. Jacob Lowman* was no better. I started a letter to louisa today No. 25.

*22:** Sateurday. we drew rations for 8 days & I had to isue them to the company. it was very hot. my boil hurt me very much. we had a very hard rain. I got a letter from louisa

23: this was a very pleasant day. their was a scout went out from the 4th Iowa to hunt a ford on the river, big black river, we receaved orders to turn over our old horses

24: Bridgeport. this morning we started to vicksburg with our horses. Co. M turned over 8 horses. I went along. it was a very hot day & vicksburg is a stinken place. I saw 5 darkies laying at the graveyard dead & not buried

25: this is a very cool morning, cool enough to wear a coat. very comfortable. the sick call has just now blowed & I must go over to the docks with the sick report

26: Wednesday. this was a very cool morning. I baked bread today & allso a lot of pies. the day was very pleasant

27: letter No. 26. very cold. last eavening cold enough through the night for frost. nothing of importence. in camp one of Co. H men died. I rote a letter to louisa s. Gantz

28: weather still cool of mornings. it rained very hard today & rained all the afternoon. I rote a letter to uncle Adam Gantz

29: cool & cloudy this morning but it cleared of through the day

30: bridgeport. last night was a very cool night. I was over at the hospital & set up with the sick. their was one co. I man that was crazy all night. he was afraid the secesh was a going to shoot him. he had been a prisiner. we had preaching at 4 oc

31: this is a very beautiful morning but it was very cold last night. part of the teams have gone after forage & the rest after rations. this afternoon rations was issued for 5 days

September 1863

1: this is a very fine day. the 2 batallion came in about noon. I baked bread. their was a scout went out from this reg for one day. all the 4th iowa came to camp but Co. M & H. Robert Young* returned from home on a furlow

2: bridgeport. I baked to day. this was a very pleasant morning, warmer than it has been for some time. we drew rations for the boys that was out on the scout to last to the 5th of this month. Co. M and H has not got in yet

3: this morning very warm & pleasant. Co. M came in to day at noon very tiered & hungery. they had been stuck on a sand bar. we drew 2 months pay 26

4: this day we lay in camp. done nothing of importence

5: this was a very pleasant morning. the whole regiment went across black river after forage for our horses. we got a good lot of sweet potatoes. it was very hot through the day

6: letter No. 28th. this was a very warm day. Lowman* died. I went to the depo after the coffon. 2 men started home on a furlow E.G. Dear [Dearduff] * & T. H. Shopmon [Shoopman].* rained in the eavening

6: [should be 7 but he labeled it 6 again] this was a very warm day. we went after forage & got more sweet potatoes. sent eleven doll & a gold pen to lou

7 [8]: bridgeport. this was a very warm day. I was very sick but it was nothing but a bad cold

8 [9]: very warm. I baked for the company. I feel considerable better than I did yesterday

10: very warm. the regiment was out after forage. found plenty of corn. nothing of importence going on to day

11: this was a very warm day. nothing of importence going on to day

12: very warm. the regiment went out after forage. got plenty acrost black river. got in about 3 oc

13: this was a very warm day. I was to the 30th iowa. several of the boys was very sick. Joseph Franklin was very sick, not expected to live

14: Shermon. very hot. we stand in nead of rain very bad. nothing of importence going on. 3 furlow men came in haris [Harris]* williams* & lowery*

15: letter No. 28th. nothing of importence going on to day in camp. I baked bread & pies. I allso rote a letter to louisa

16: not strange weather. very hot & dry

17: camp sherman. this eavening it rained & through the night it got very cold—to cool to be plesent. com M. was out on picket for the first time for a long while

18: very cold all day. the boys went out for a scout. came in about noon. saw some rebils but did not get any

19: last night was very cool. some of the boys nearly froze. very cool all day. I baked today

20: bridgeport. very cool but pleasant. boots & sadles blowed at noon. the boys all sadled & went out without anything to eat or sleep on & it was very cold & they did not get back untill next day & they nearly froze

21: letter No. 29th. this was a very cool day. the boys did not get in untill after dinner. I had to bake bread & pies. I rote a letter to louisa S. Gantz but did not get any & was very much disapointed

22: this was another very fine day. their is nothing of

importence going. we lay in camp. I rote a letter to Reebeca H. Patten

23: warm & pleasant. I baked 2 to & a lot of pies. no mail yet

24: letter No. 30. very pleasant but cool nights. we are at camp sherman near bridgeport. I rote a letter to louisa

25: very pleasant. nothing of importence going on in camp. Co. M was on picket

26: bridgeport camp sherman. this was a very pleasant day. I was very busy. I baked 2 & a lot of pies

27: very pleasant. I did not do very much. the cave. went out on a 4 day scout

28: C. Sherman. cool & cloudy. we have orders to move our camp

29: camp sherman. very pleasant. we was expecting to move camp all day but this eavening the orders came that we would not move so we was all glad of it

30: camp sherman. very cool nights but pleasant days. some of our boys are on pickets & some on scout. I am still baking

October 1863

1: camp sherman. very cool this morning. it rained all night last nite. no mail yet. the boys came in to day off of the scout. saw a great many rebs & brought some in

[NOTE: Entries for October 2, 3, and 4 have a big X through them.]

2: very pleasant cool night. the teams went to the river after forage. very dry. we nead rain. very pleasant. nothing of importence

3: letter No. 31. this day is very pleasant. I was very busy for I had to bake 2 & a lot of pies. I rote a letter to lou. Com. H was on picket today & was fiered into by some gorillies but done no harm

4: very pleasant. I did not do anything today. Co. M went out on a scout with the rest of the cav command. I rote a letter for Sameyl How [Howe]*

5: camp sherman. very pleasant. Co. M on picket. very cooll nights. one of our boys started home on a sick furlow Lemon Chester*

6: very pleasant. still very cool. nothing of importence. we are laying in camp building shanties and stables

7: No. 32. last night night it rained all night. this day was cloudy untill about noon then cleared of & was prety & I rote a letter to Louisa S. Gantz. letter No. 32

8: very pleasant but cool

9: very pleasant but very cool nights. nothing of importence going on in camp

10: very pleasant. nothing of importence. Eli [Dearduff]* returned this eavening about 4 oclock. the pickets on the north post was drove into camp this afternoon. we are expecting an attact here every moment

11: sherman. letter No. 33. this is a very beautiful day. we have been expecting an atact today but the thing has kind of blowed away this eavening so I rote a letter to lou

12: nothing of importence. Co. M is on picket. weather cool & pleasant

13: Com returned from on picket all rite. it rained some through the night

14: camp sherman. very cool & pleasant. we are still laying in the same old camp sherman

15: this day their was a large scout started out for 8 days about 14 thousand. I loaned eli [Dearduff]* 2 dollars. we allso mooved camp to the depo

16: camp depo. very pleasant but cool. I did not get to camp until 11 oc. then I built a bake oven. I loaned rowe* 20 dollars

17: depo. we are here in the convalescent camp not doing very much. all that I have to do is bake

18: this is a very fine day. their was two of our boys returned from furlow shopman [Shoopman]* & G. Thompson.* it rained very hard last night

19: letter no. 34. I went to the depo & allso to the out picket post to get some fresh butter. I loaned 5 dollars to S. kirkpatrick.* I rote a letter to louisa—r. kirk paid

20: very pleasant. the scout came in this eavening. had

considerable of fighting while they was out. they lost 1 man prisoner S.R. White*

21: very pleasant. we moved camp went back to our old camp sherman. found things all right. I baked before I moved

22: this morning looked some like rain. we had to move camp within 8 miles of vicksburg. I did not get in till after dark & it rained that night some

23: very cool. I mad an oven today. it rained nearly all day. I got 2 old letters from lou

24: very cool today. I baked in the new oven & it done fine

25: this was a very pleasant day but I had to work very hard but did not like to work on sunday. we got our pay for 2 months 26 dollars

26: letter no. 35. this was a very nice day. Co. M was on a scout. No. 5 build a shebang. I rote a letter to louisa after bed time. Miss wood [Woods]* is here to night

27: this was a very pleasant day. we got a large lot of sanitaries to camp & Mrs. Woods is here yet & going to stay till tomorrow

28: this was a very warm day. Co. M went on picket. Mrs. Woods started home today & I sent 60 dollars with her to father, allso a letter to pa. I rec a letter from R. Paten

29: very pleasant. this morning about it commenced raining & rained all the afternoon. I built me a bake shebang

30: rained very hard last night. is still raining today. I did not do very much onley baked batch of bread for the company

31: this was a very beautiful day. it cleared off & was very pleasant. I baked 1 batch of bread & 2 of pies. 2 of our boys started home on furlows Andy Dunn* & M. B. Sheafor.* the 4 iowa was on a scout last night

November 1863

1: this was a very beautiful day. I am resting & came to the notion that I would rite to louisa so I am now riting. I allso rot a letter for How [Howe]*

2: this was a very nice day. nothing of importence

3: very pleasant. still in camp near vicksburg at clear creek

4: we are camped at clear creek. Com. M was on picket today. very pleasant

5: this is a very rainy day. nothing going on of importence

6: rained last night. still raining today. cleared off this morning. today is very pleasant. I got a letter from louisa & eta

7: this is a very fine day. the infantry moved away from here. the cav was out on a scout. some of Co. M was on gard

8: letter no. 37th. this was a very beautiful day. we had preaching in the regiment. I rote a letter to louisa & sent her 50 cts

9: camp clearcreek. nothing of importence. I received a letter from louisa

10: very pleasant. 15 of company M was on picket

11: last night was a very cool night. 10 more of Com M are on picket to day. this day is very pleasant. we drew rations for 10 days

12: very pleasant. nothing going on in camp of importence

13: Camp Clearcreek. weather pleasant Com. M was on a scout & did not get in untill 12 oc at night. Peck [Alexander] Majors* went to the hospital as we caried him their

14: this morning the orderly started home recruiting. this was a very pleasant day

15: letter no. 38. this was a very nice day. we had preaching at 2 oc in the afternoon. it was a very good sermon. I rote a letter to louisa

16: this was a very pleasant day. we are still in camp at clearcreek. nothing of importence going in camp. mail came in but I got no letter

17: this was a very pleasant morning. 5 of Co. M on pickets. I am baking today but I do not feel very well on the account of a cold that I have

18: well this was a very pleasant day. the rest of Com. M was on picket. some of them mounted & some dismounted. ike turner* came back to the com after being gone nearly 2 years

19: letter No. 39. warm & pleasant. about noon the boys came in off of picket. cloudy this eavening & looks very much like rain. I am riting to louisa tonight

20: I received a letter from lou last night. it rained some through the night. still misten some to day. we received 2 months pay today about noon. allso drew 10 days rations

21: this was a very pleasant day. I did not bake any thing but pies for we did not draw very much flour. the col. made a speach this eavening to the reg. to get them to enlist as vetran soldiers

22: i rote some to lous. very cool last night but through the day it is very warm & pleasant. we had preaching this afternoon at 2 oc. tonight at 8 oc the regiment was ordered on a scout

23: the morning was cloudy, misted some the fore noon. the boys did not get in off of the scout untill afternoon & they was tiered & hungery for they did not have anything to eat nor did not get to sleep any

24: last night it rained very hard nearly all night. this morning 2 of Com. M went on picket. about noon it cleared off & was a very prety day over head

25: last night was very cool but very clear & moon shiney. this morning it is very pleasant but some cool

26: very cool last night. tolerable pleasant today. nothing going on in camp

27: very pleasant but some cloudy all day. their was 2 brigades of infantry came out here

28: last night rained some nearly all night & is still raining some this morning. this eavening their was 6 recruits came to this Co. this was my birthday & I worked hard all day

29: last night was the coldest night that we have had down this far dixi & it is cool all day today. we did not have any preaching but had aple dumplings for dinner

30: this was a very beautiful day. I was very busy today making pies for the infantry. it was very cool last night. this eavenin our boys went out on a scout to the Yazoo to cature a boat with some rebs on but did not get them

December 1863

1: this was a very nice day. I did not bake any for I was out of material. I went to the depo after a new supply but did not get what I wanted so I had to return disapointed. not going on of importence

    2: very heavy frost last night but very pleasant today. Com M is on picket. today we had 2 of our boys to return Chester* & dunn.* I sent & got a barl of flour today & I am baking pies this eavening

    3: this was a very fine morning. all of the wagons went after forage. 4 men went from Com. M. 2 of our boys returned off of furlow Dunn* & Chester*

    4: this morning their was a large scout went out for 5 or 6 days. 18 men went from Co. M. this was a very nice day. one furlow man returned M.V.B. Sheafor.* a large mail this eavening

    5: very pleasant today. nothing of importence going on at this place. we are still in the old camp on clearcreek

    6: letter no. 41st. warm & pleasant. this is a very beautiful day. we had preaching & speaking from the Col. this eavening at 2 oc the Col. spoke in regard to the reinlisting of the old soldiers in the vetrans

    7: warm & pleasant but some cloudy. I do not feel very well on the account of a very bad cold but I am as to be about & doing well

    8: last night it rained very hard. this morning it was some mudy but through the day it cleared up & is now very pleasant

    9: letter no. 42nd. this is a very fine day. great excitement amongst the vetrans. I did not do anything for my mind was troubled so that I could not. so this eavening warner* & I put down our names then we rote home to our women

    10: very warm & pleasant. nothing of importence going on in camp. we are still in camp on clearcreek Miss. their was a very large mail came into camp & I rec. a letter from louisa

    11*: camp clearcreek. warm & cloudy, misting some by intervills. nothing of importence. this eavening we was caled out in line to receive some instruction as vetrans & allso to take the oath of illegence. I rec a letter from lou

    12: warm & pleasant, but still cloudy. it rained some last night. this morning Co. M drew some new horses. we are in camp at clearcreek. nothing of importence going on

    13: letter no. 43rd. last night it was cloudy & rained very hard untill about noon then it cleared off. then we had speaking. this afternoon I rote a letter to louisa & put 2 dollars in it

14: this is a very beautiful day. trade is very dull. I am not doing anything. the scout has not returned yet. we are looking for them deily

15: very pleasant some cloudy

16: last night it rained very hard. some of Co. M was on picket. it rained very hard all day. we did not do very much. this eavening it cleared off

17: this day was very cool but clear. about noon the scout came in about noon after being out 10 days but they did not have very much to do

18: very pleasant but some cool all day, about the clearest cool day we have had since last winter. we drew some more ney horses. the camp is nearly full of horses now

19: this is a very beautiful day. last night was very heavy frost but the day is pleasant. the com is not doing any thing onley lying in camp & am not doing anything onley baking once

20: letter no. 44th. this is a very beautiful morning. we had preaching at 2 oc, that was all that was going on in camp. I rote a letter to louisa this eavening

21: very warm & beautiful. I baked pies & bread to day. old man byers* started home. I drew 2 lotery tickets valued at 15 dol & started them of with 2 30 cent in for which I am to get a gold locket & a set of lades jewelry

22: warm & pleasant but some cloudy. nothing of importence going on in camp onley the boys are fighting a sham batel with clubs & brickbats

23: very pleasant. nothing of importence going on. this regiment got about 150 recruits Com M got 8 of them [the next line was written then scratched out] this was Christmas eave & the boys had a prety big time

24: very pleasant. nothing going on of importence. this is as beautiful a Christmas eave as I ever saw & the boys are having quite a time. Co. H was sworen in as vetrans

25: this was a very fine day. we had a big aple dumpling dinner today. we allso had a oyster supper this eavening. Com L had a big spree this eavening but they had to quile

26: very warm & pleasant. nothing going on at presant. this eavening was some cloudy. looks very much like rain

27: letter No. 45. last night was a very rainy night & today it is raining all day. nothing of importence going on in this reg. a quite a acident hapend in the 10 Mo., one man shot his brother. this eavening I rote a letter to louisa

28: last night cleared off very nice & this is a very pleasant day but some cool. nothing of importence going on. I received a letter from louisa, No.42

29: very pleasant. still in camp on clear creek. nothing going of importence going on

30: some cloudy today. rained some in the afternoon

31: last night it rained all night & is still raining today. their is not very much excitement about new years yet for it has turned very cool

1864

January 1864

JACOB GANTZ used a narrow, black book for his writings in early 1864 although the front of the book has the following information:"Daily Register 1857 for the use of private families and persons of business—containing a blank for every day in the year, for the record of interesting daily occurrences and future engagements."

1: last night was the first snow we have had in these parts & today is very cool. this eavening we elected our officers Capt. Whitney,* 2nd Lieu M. Sheafer [Sheafor]*
2: today the weather was more pleasant. some of Com. M was on picket. the Cap got a keg of ale & several of the boys got very funney for it was stronger than they expected
3: this is a very pleasant day. we had preaching at 2 oc. I allso rote a letter to louisa
4: last night was a very rainey night & their was 20 of Com M on picket. it has been raining all day & it is a very mudy time but is now very cold
[No entry for January 5]
6: This was a very nice day but some cold after the rain

49

yesterday & last night. This evening is lonely & looks like it was going to snow. We are in camp at Clear Creek.

7: Last night it rained some through the night but not very hard today. was some cloudy & cool but not so cold as it was yesterday. no sty in camp only about going home as vetrans

8: We are lying in camp on Clear Creek. Noting of importence going on but it is very cold.

9: Still cold. We are signing the payrolls. the teams has been to Vicksburg after 10 days rations.

10: Letter No. 47. This is a very beautiful morning. We had team inspection at 8 oc. At 3 we had preaching. Towards eavening it cloud up & rained some. I roted a letter to lou. orders came for 20 men to go for a scout for 3 days to start at 5 in the morning.

11: This morning at 5 the scout started out. nothing, nothing of importance going. it rained some.

12: The scout returned but did not get any thing for the roads was muddy.

13: This is a very pleasant day. last eavening I received a letter from louisa No. 41st. today about noon the scout returned. the did not go very far on account of bad roads.

14: This has been a very beautiful day. This eavening it is warm & some cloudy. I am now siting in my bake house wating for the oven to cool for to put a batch of bread in & now it is ready. one recruit to Co. M. today.

15: Very warm & pleasant. We are in camp Clear Creek. nothing of importence going on. only making rings of the tree where Grant* & Pemberton* met when Vicksburg was surrendered

16: This is a very beautiful morning. nothing of importence occurred.

17: very pleasant morning. we had preaching at 3 oc. This eavening about dark it begin to rain & it rained very hard until about 9 oc

18: letter no. 48. this morning was very pleasant. it was nearly cleared off. we had some discouraging about the vetrans going home. I was very much discouraged. rote a letter to lou.

19: nothing of importence. this morning things look more favorable than they did yesterday. the roads are mudy on the acount of the hard rain.

20: nothing of importence. we are drawing ten days more rations.

21: This is a very beautiful day & I was very lucky for when the mail came in I got 2 letters from home dated Jan. 3 & 8. lou said that she did not want me to reinlist but it was too late.

22: very warm & pleasant. nothing of importence going on. no pay yet. we have been looking for our pay every day for near one month. These are the pretyest nights I ever saw.

23: This morning looks allmost like spring. we had to polease our quarters. we have now cleaned all rite & I am siting by the table riting. I did not do one thing today only bake one batch of bread and rested the balance of the time.

24: letter no. 48. this was a very nice day. nothing of importence going on. we had service at 3 oc. I allso rote a letter to louisa. letter num. 48th

25: very warm & pleasant. things are very dull in camp on the account of going home as vetrans. I rote a letter for Sameul how [Howe]* & put 15 dollars in it.

26: this day Co. M is on picket. their is allso a train & escort started out after forage to be gone 9 days

27: The forage train that went out yesterday returned before noon & was chaced some by the bushwackers. the escort came in about 1 oc. they wounded one secesh & got 3 horses and lots of corn

28: this is a very warm & nice day. we had regimental inspection at 9 oc & inspection of quarters at 2 oc. this eavening they are paying of the reg tonight at 9 oc. we got our pay. I rec. 195 dolars.

29: this day is warm & pleasant. the rest of the soldiers are getting their pay now but the vetrans got pay yesterday.

30: this is a very warm day. I have been very busy. I baked 450 lbs. of bread and 65 pies.

31: letter no. 50. this day is some cloudy. I am still busy baking, fixing for the boys to eat out on the scout which they are expected to start on tomorrow. I allso rote a letter to lou

February 1864

1: last night it rained some but this morning is pleasant. the scout did not get started. we drew 10 days rations for the Co. and 3 days for the scouts.

2: this is a very pleasant morning. the scout has not started yet but are looking for orders every moment

3: this morning the scout started out. their was allso troops trapsing all day last night. logstan [Logsdon]* of Co. M died. our boys had some fighting to do. got some killed and some wounded.

4: troops are still passing. the rebs are fleeing before our men and well they may for we are going to chace them through today at noon. I started to Vicksburg to lay in a stock

5: I got to Vicksburg late. did not get any thing last night so today I had a great deal of running around & then did not get what I wanted. but I got some fish & a bbl. of flour and got back to camp about 3 oc and was tiered.

6: This is a very pleasant day but some windy. I am not doing very much for I am near out of can flour. we have not heard from the advance of the army today. one of our boys started on a furlow of shootmen.

7: letter sent no. 51. warm & pleasant. we had preaching today in our new church but I did not get to go for I was busy baking. I allso rote a letter to Lou.

8: warm and pleasant. nothing of importence going on in camp. we are still in camp Clearcreek, Miss.

9: we heard of the scout today. they are still getting along fine. had several fights but nary defeat

10: warm & pleasant. nothing of importence only we are having a meeting going on. several have joined.

11: this is a very beautiful day. I am not doing very much only baking some. Wm. Carson* came in this eavening from Iowa.

12: warm & pleasant. nothing of importence going on in camp. we had very good meeting tonight.

13: very pleasant. still in Camp Clearcreek. their is no meeting this eavening.

14: letter no. 57. this is a very beautiful sabath. we had morning meeting at 9 & preaching at 2 this afternoon & service this eavening at early candle light. I allso rote a letter to lou.

15: last night it rained very hard toward morning. their was 27 joined the church. I allso got a letter from louisa

16: letter no. 52. this was a very pleasant day but some cooler than we have had for some time. I rote a letter to louisa.

17: last night it snowed & I got prety cold & it is very cool all day today.

18: last night was I think one of the coldest nights we have had but it is clear today but very cool.

19: very pleasant but still cool. nothing of importence going on in camp of importence. only some of the boys are drinking too much ail.

20: more pleasant last night. the darkies held meeting in our church. they formed a class & several of them joined.

21: this day is very warm & pleasant we had meeting this morning at 8 & allso this afternoon at 2 oc. allso preaching at night. Thomas McConahs [McConnaughey]* returned from off a furlow.

22: letter no. 53. very pleasant. nothing going on in camp of importence. I rote a letter to Louisa S. Gantz.

23: rather cool nighs but pleasant through the day. we are still in Camp Clearcreek or rather Camp Heborn, we are camped on the old Heborn farm.

24: still pleasant but not very much doing in camp

25: their are about half of our boys drunk on ail. they get it at the teamsters mess. I rec. a letter from louisa S. gantz.

26: letter no. 54. very pleasant last night. their was a dispatch came in from the scout to gen tuttle.* our boys are at Canton returning.

27: this was a fine day. I had to work very hard fixing for the boys. when they would come in Co. H came in last night.

28: very beautiful morning. I was fixing for church at 9 when our boys returned they did not get to go but I went at 9 oc & night.

March 1864

1: this morning was rather misty. I went to the depo to get some bakeries. I came back & went to baking like as if I was in earnest.

2: last night it rained very hard & is still raining this morning. recruit came for Co. M

3: it has cleared of & is a very fine day. the scout returned today. we have orders to start home in the morning

4*: this morning we are getting ready to start home. some of them are gone. this is a very nice morning. this eaevening we are lying on the Constitution at Vicksburg. some cloudy

5: last night was a very pleasant night. this morning we are still on the boat at Vicksburg. we left town today at 2 oc. I received a letter from louisa

6: this is a very pleasant day. we are on our way home on the Constitution but we are going very slow. we are allso on upper deck.

7: last night was some cool but we fared well for we had plenty of blankets. we had sermon today abord

8: this morning we got to helena about 7 oc. I eat breakfast with willcox [Wilcox].* I allso saw Col. Brooks. we are now bound for Memphis. did not stay more than a half of an hour at helena.

9: we are now traveling a prety good rate. this morning at 8 we got to Memphis. their we laid untill noon. then started out for cairo. we are going a little faster than we did yesterday.

10: this morning is some cloudy in the afternoon. wind very high. rained some this eaevening. we landed several times to wood. this night is so dark that we have to run very slow

11: this morning was some cloudy but very pleasant. we got to Cairo about 2 oc. laid their about 3 hours 3 Com got off. we started on for st. louis. while in cairo we had some fun with their reg.

12: this morning it is very cool just about as cool weather as we have. say we are a long the free states lines & we begin to feel like were most home.

COMPANY *muster roll in military records said Jacob Gantz was sick at home after April 14, 1864; pension records said he was ill in Iowa during March and April 1864. Gantz commented when he began his next diary that he had been home on veteran's furlough. On the front of the brown diary is an easy to read "J. S. Gantz." But by turning the book to the light, one can read the etching— now barely visible—"Jacob S. Gantz's book Do not steal it for fear of shame"*

Dear Book of 1864
Belonging to Jacob S. Gantz of Co. M of the 4th Iowa vetron vol cav.
I bought this book in Cairo on the 3rd day of May 1864 while on the downward trip to my regiment after being home 43 days on vetron furlow. my home is at Brookville, Jefferson Co. Iowa. have a wife and one child living at Brookville. any one finding this book will please give it to the owner or send it to my home & will be rewarded.

Although Jacob said he bought it on May 3, 1864, the first entry is dated April 28, 1864. At the end of the furlough, the more than five hundred men from the Fourth Iowa Cavalry who had been home were to reassemble at Davenport, Iowa, to begin the return south, according to the regimental history. Apparently Gantz was in Iowa a couple of weeks longer—and his military records indicated that he may have been ill—thus his return south to join his regiment was somewhat different. He rejoined his regiment at Memphis, Tennessee, where it had been ordered from the Vicksburg, Mississippi, area, to go to be reequipped and readied for another arduous campaign.

April 1864

28: this morning I left home, got on the cars at fairfield, went to Otunway, lay their 4 hours then started for kokuk. got their at half past 8 oc. put up at the smith house & soon after was sound asleep
29: this morning we tried to get transportation but could not in time to go on the morning packet so we payed our way down to St. Louis
30: letter No. 1 rec. this morning we got to St. louis at 7 but

could not leave that day so I went out to see the 9th iowa & stayed all night I rote a letter to louisa S. Gantz

May 1864

1*: This morning I came into st. lou & Row [Rowe]* had not got transportation yet & we could not get untill tomorrow. so I concluded I wanted got to memphis & wate untill they come & got on the boat with Co. G abord the Henry ames. the boys had a pass with the poleaseamen. we left at 2 oc

2: we are on the henry ames. we got to cairo a 2 oc. I was looking to go out this eavening but did not get off on some account

3: letter no. 2 rec. we did not get to leave cairo untill today at 1 oc. then the boat launched for memphis. I rote a letter to louisa and left it at Cairo

4: last night we run all night. past Fort Pillow this morning about 7 oc & got to memphis at 3 oc. the boat was going to lay their 3 hours so I got off & found that our reg. had came up. so I got off of the boat & came out to the reg which was 1 mile out of town but the most of the boys was on a scout had started on sateurday last. me & the 3 Iowa cav are camped togeather

5: this morning I was put on duty & was on all day drawing rations for the reg. we have very warm weather

6: letter no. 3 rec. this was a very nice day. I lay in camp & rote louisa a letter

7: very pleasant but warm. I walked down to town & went near all over the town & got very tiered. the 1st Iowa Cave went through town this eavening

8: letter no. 4 rec. this was a very nice day. I was to preeching then afternoon I rote a letter to louisa

9: willcox [Wilcox]* stayed with us last night. this eavening it rained but it was very hot & dusty before

10: last night it rained prety hard. this is a very pleasant day but it is some showery

11: letter no. 5 rec. last night it rained very hard. the scout came in this eavening & our Co. is the largest now it ever was. I rote a letter to lou

12: nothing of importence going on in camp. we are still at memphis. this is a very nice day

13: we are still in camp at Memphis. we had orders to clean up for inspection tomorow. we allso had dres praid & I was on gard

14: this is a very nice morning. we are prepareing for inspection. we had inspection at 9 & did not get in untill 12. we had a very large & nice looking reg

15: letter no. 6. this is a very nice day but very warm. I rote a letter to louisa S. Gantz

16: this is a very hot day & allso very dusty. I rote a letter to Rebeca Paten

17: I rote to Esther. this was a very pleasant day. nothing going on in camp

18: very hot. I found several old acquaintence in the 15 Ohio Co. C

19: letter no. 7th rec. this was a very hot day. we moved camp about a mile then I rote a letter to lou

20: this was a very nice day. we are still in camp at memphis. we fixed up our camp. lieut sheafor* started home today

21: this was a very hot day. I was on horse gard. I rec. a letter from louisa s. gantz

22: lay in camp. letter no. 8. it is very warm & dusty

23: this eavening we had some appearence of rain but did not get any. I rec a letter from louisa s. gantz

24: very pleasant. their was a picknic near here. it was a Gearman school

25: very hot. I was down to town on a pass. nothing of importence going on

26: letter no. 9 rec. still in camp. I was on a stable gard today

GANTZ becomes one of a reconnoitering force of 1,500 men who ride many miles in search of the enemy. There are many scouting trips at this time, but few encounters with the enemy.

27: this morning at 3 oc we started on a scout. I did not get back untill 8 oc at night. we rode over 40 miles & it was very dry & dusty. it was a very hard day on me

28: I was down to see the 3rd Iowa boys. will [Gantz]* was hurt. I drew my pay on my furlow

29: letter no. 10. this was a very warm day. I rote a letter to lou. we started out on a scout to night at 10 oc

30: this morng we was about 24 miles from campe at a little town by the name of Hernando. about 12 we started back. got to camp at 10 oc at night. we had a very dusty scout & it was allso very hot

31: letter no. 11th. we lay in camp today & rested. this was a very hot day. I rote a letter to louisa this eavening. we rec. scouting orders to start in the morning

June 1864

1: we started this morning. it was very hot dry & dusty. at 3 oc we had a very heavy rain & thunderstorm. lasted about 1 hour then it moderated some. we camped at Collersvile 25 miles from Memphis & it rained all night on us

2: we marched 5 miles then we halted in woolf river botoms at layfayett. lay their untill 5 oc then we marched untill 12 oc all night. then we camped & was very sleepy, wet and tiered

3: we marched about 6 oc. about the time we started it begin to rain & it rain by spells all day. we camped at 3 oc. a detail went after corn for the horses. just as we got a place fixed to sleep it begin to rain & rained all night. we had some fresh hog for our supper

4: we started at 7 oc. at noon we fed our horses & rested one hour. then we went 3 miles. came to salom, went one mile further, camped for the nite. got some forage for our horses, killed some beef, lived pretty well, generally. it rained through the day but none at night

5: we did not start untill 10 oc. then we went 2 miles & stoped, killed some more beef. I drew & issued to the com. we allso drew rations. at sundown we marched again. did not stop untill 12 oc. it did not rain any today or tonite

6: this morning we had a very heavy rain & thunder storm. after it had rained about 1 hour, we started & it rained untill noon when the sun came out & looked very nice. we rested 1 hour & eat some hardtack & sowbely. we went on 3 miles camped at Rackersville. the 3rd batallion went after forage & did not get in untill after night

CONFEDERATE General Forrest had assembled a force of more than ten thousand soldiers in this area with the intent of recapturing Memphis, Tennessee. The Fourth Iowa Cavalry encountered a scouting party of the Rebels and suffered some losses before continuing their expedition.

7: we did not start untill today noon. about 4 our advance run into the rebs & the rebs retreated back to hache river which was 8 miles from ripley. their is where (blur) Henderson of the 3rd iowa got killed. some of the 4 got wounded & we allso lost some of our horses. we camped near the hache river. it rained some through the day

8: this morning it is raining pretty hard. we did not leave our camp untill afternoon. then we drew rations & the cav went 1 road & train & infantry the other & I went with the train as I was not very well. we camped at 4 & 1 hour after the cav came alone & went past

9: they are making preparation to send some of the train & the sick back to memphis. they did not get off untill noon. I went with them as I was sick to gard prisiners. we had 24. we passed through ripley, marched 12 miles & camped for the nite. it rained nearly all nite

AGAIN, Confederate General Forrest's strong forces were encountered at Brice's Cross Roads, six miles from Guntown, Mississippi. This resulted in heavy losses for the Union force. According to the regimental history, the Fourth Iowa Cavalry was in the saddle for fifty-four consecutive hours with no provisions for the men or their horses.

10: this morning started prety early. went through salom, 5

miles further & camped. we marched 15 miles. at 10 the force that went on got into a fight & fought 7 hours & had to retreat with a very heavy loss. lost all their train & artillery but 2 peaces & nearly all the infantry but the cav got out by hard fiting

11: we started at 6. it rained some through the day. we got to layfayette 1 hour by sun & camped at 10 oc at night. the retreating soldrers begin to come along. they have been fighting all day very hard. they made a stand this morning at ripley

12: Last night we started at 12 oc. when we started the road was lined with retreating soldiers & teamsters. nearly all the teamsters got away by cuting a mule out & skedadleing. the road was lined all day with men coming in, some walking & some riding give out horses. I got to camp at noon & was sick. I rode 30 miles today

13: I am in camp winslow & I am very sick. I rote a letter to Martha [Dearduff].* the rest of the Co is not here yet but are at Jearmantown station. they are resting & waching the rebs

14: letter no. 12. in Camp Winslow. we are not doing anything. the boys came in the eavening. I rec. a letter from louisa

15: lay in camp. I am on stable gard

16: resting in Camp Winslow

17: we are building ovens for the reg. I was to preeching this eavening. lovejoy preached.

CAMP WINSLOW

18: I am working at our oven. I am not very well but as weak as a cat

19: we had monthley inspection. I helped bake this morning. this is a very hot day. this eavening ingles lectured to us on the subject of the orphans home

20: letter No. 13. this was a very nice day. I signed 2 dollars to the orphans home. I received a letter from lou

21: laying in Camp Winslow. it rained some today. we have orders for a scout to go out to see Forest. We not know when we will go but I suppose before very long

22: it rained some last night & is cloudy & rainy some this morning. this afternoon we drew our pay. I drew 17.65 cts. I then collected some & then expressed 110 dollars home to father by whiting*

23: letter no. 14. this morning I went to town with a squad of men to get notions. I bought a album & some paper. I rote a letter to lou S. Gantz. I was to preaching last night

AFTER ten days rest, another expedition moved south toward Tupelo with the purpose of pursuing Confederate General Forrest's force to retaliate for the earlier heavy losses to them.

24*: this morning is very warm & clear. the scout starts out this morning at 8 oc. went as far as Gearmantown & camped

25: we marched at 6 oc. passed through layfayet at 3 oc then went 5 miles further 2 miles on wollf river & camped for the night

26: this morning we moved back acrossed Woolf river & camped - very warm - in the afternoon drew rations. just at sundown we started for legrange. got their at 12 oc 10 miles & camped in an orcherd

27: we lay in camp at legrange all day. it is very warm. the cars came in to day about noon. we had all the potatoes & fresh meet aples & other vegetables we wanted to eat. some of the boys cleaned out one sulter

28: we left legrange this morning at 4 oc. passed through grand junction at 6. got to sallsbury 10 oc which was 10 miles from legrange. their we camped. Co K saw 10 or 12 rebs but they left. very warm but not dusty

29: we are still in camp at Sollsbury. very hot looked some like rain but did no. Co. M killed 2 very nice hogs & had some good rosts & stews

30: letter no. 15. sollsbury have nothing to do onley coock & tend to our horses. but it is so hot that it is enough to do that the thermomiter stands at 102. I rote to louisa

July 1864

1: lay in camp. drew feed for 2 days. very hot. we received mail. none for me

2: this morning Co. M went on picket. I went out on post with 6 men. stood cloce to a house where their was 4 secesh women. we got our dinner their & got a very good dinner & supper

3: myself & releaf fell back to the reserve last night. I got to rest all night. went out on post this mor at 4 oc. was releaved at 8 oc. went in to camp. fed our horses. got something to eat. lay down to take a nap. had not slept more than 2 hours when our pickets was fired on & boot & sadles blowed. in 15 minutes we was out in line of batle. we was out untill about 10 oc at night but did not see any more rebs so we went into camp at another place west of sallsbury

4: last night after geting into camp I slept very sound for I was very sleepy. we lay in camp all day. at noon a train came out brought us our spencer carbines. some of our boys came along as detail to gard the train through. in the afternoon their was 11 men & the cap came to reinforce us. we sent out in the country and got us a lot of potatoes chickens & other things cabitch beets & c. & had a regular good dinner of which I eat very harty fo I was hungry.

5: letter no. 16th. very warm. I washed my shirt & drawers & went without untill they dried. the train came out at 10 oc. some of our boys went back on it. I rote a letter to louisa S. G. it rained this eavening at 5 oc. just at dark we received marching orders & in 1 hour we was on the march. we went through sollsbury then marched 10 miles south & camped in a very bushey place

6: did not march this morning. about 12 we had a nice little shour. at 1 oc we marched. went 12 miles without seeing any rebs to amount to anything & camped for the night & I rested fine for I was begining to get waried some

7: very warm this morning. I was on horse gard last night. their was 2 or 3 shots fired on picket through the night. the 3rd brigade passed us this morning & went in the advance. today they was skirmishing all day with the enemy. this afternoon they run aganst the enemy in force & the 2nd iowa dismounted & fought them about 3 hours & drove them killing 11 & wounding 27. the day being very hot, the boys gave out & the 4th iowa got orders to dismount & we done so but when we got their the enemy was on the retreat & we followed them 1 mile & a half & did not get a shot. then we was ordered back 1 mile to camp for the night. it rained a hard shour

8: last night 2 reg of cav came to reinforce us & some of our boys came along. they brought me 3 letters. last night we camped in 2 miles of ripley on a creek. we found where several of our men had been buried that was killed on the stuigis [General Sturgis] retreat & their had just been a little hole dig & them thrown in & the hogs had dug them up & eat them & their bones was laying around the hole. started this morning at sunup. passed through ripley. marched 4 miles further. rested, fed & got something to eat. we was on the left flank today. came in to the rest of the cav & the infantry one hour by sun & camped for the night. I saw Noah Ness at that place

9: we marched this morning at sunup on the road to tupilow. at noon we came to a little town new allbany 12 miles. their we camped Co. M & 1 Co. of the 3rd iowa went out on picket. Co. M had to petroll the road. we went out one time 5 miles on a rod where their was supposed to be a large force but we did not see any of the scamps. our picket post was rite in a blackbury patch & we had plenty of blackburies, aples, potatoes & chickens to eat while we was on picket that night. had a nice time for picket but did not get to sleep very much for it was aganst orders as the enemy was near.

10: started this morning 4 oc. marched 5 miles. the advance fired on some reb pickets, stoped & rested untill our forces a got togeather, then started out 4th iowa in the advance. we skirmished for about 8 miles then we came near a little town, vary croose, where we run aganst a pretty large force. had a pretty hard fight with them but the enemy retreated. we followed after them about 3 miles & camped for the night. it was then noon. I was among the detail to go after foreage. we get plenty for our horses to eat. this was a very hot day. I suffered very much with the heat. some cloudy. looks like it would rain to nite

11: it rained some last night & is very cloudy this morning. we

camped in 8 miles of pontotoc. marched this morning at 4 oc. had
some fighting to do but not to amount to anything. we got to
ponttoc at 8 oc. found rebel pickets their but the armey had rtreted.
the whole force camped around the town

12: a heavy detail went out after forage from cachree. some of
them found the enemy. the 9th ill. cav got one man killed & 6
wounded. the 3rd iowa got camp men wounded. I got a jar of
butter & many other things to eat. we will remain here at pontotoc
one more night

13: very pleasant. looks some like rain. we marched this
morning at 4 oc toward tupilow which was 18 miles. the cave got
their aganst 2 oc. found but very little opposition. some skirmishing
al the way but we crowded them so cloce they had to leave 1 man
laying in the road that had stoped breathing & it is no more than
likely they caried many away with them. when we got to tupilow
their was a train of cars fast came in cite but they went back. we
then dismounted tore up 4 miles of railroad & then camped for the
night

*THE upcoming several days of battles Gantz describes put an end to the
pursuit that started after Forrest's earlier attack on the Union forces in June.*

14: last night we lay down expecting to get a good nights
sleep but at 11 oc their was a detail came to our brigade for C Co. &
their was 3 sent from the 3rd Iowa and 3 from the 4th. Co. M was
one of the camps. we went out on the pontotoc road about 2 miles,
placed the companies around in the best position could be done to
prevent the enemy of comeing in, then sent out videtts to allarm us
of any approaching enemy & the rest of us dismounted & held our
horses untill morning. just as day begin to break they sliped up &
fired on one of our videtts & wounded him. the rest of soon rallied
first mounted but the rebs had too good a chance at us & wounded
one of our horses. we then dismounted, sent our horses to the rear
& fought them 4 hours when the rebs rallied their force & charged
on us. we then fell back gradily. the last volley we fired at them
they was within 25 yds of us. the bullet flew very thick over our
heads & their was but one of our men wounded. we then fell in the
rear of the infantry & they opened on them with spirit. the rebs
charged on the but was repulsed & our men charged them, drove

them back. they retreated leaveing the ground covered with their
dead. our cav was then ordered back to the rear to prevent an
enemy from comeing in. while their we get us something to eat & a
little rest. they allso brought a great many of the where was & they
was awful looking sights. at 2 oc in the afternoon we was ordered
out to bring on another engagement. we found plenty of them in
the same place. we dismounted & had hard fighting with them for
4 or 5 hours when they mad another charge on us & we had to use
our legs very fast. when we was ordered to fall back or we would
have been cought but they did not follow us far

　15: we did not get to leave the battlefield last night untill 11
oc. then we was tiered, sleepy & hungry but was out of rations. we
lay down & slept untill 3 oc in the morning, then we sadled our
horses & lay down again & slept untill 7 oc when we was ordered
to the front. we then went to the same place on the pontotoc road
where we found the rebs thick. we did not have to skirmish with
them more than 2 hours untill they charged us in force. we then
dismounted, formed on the left of the infantry. the rebs charged on
us with all their force on our artillery & infantry & our men
repulsed them again, opened our artillery by volleys. they cut the
rebs down worse than we had the morning before. we was then
ordered back to the rear to gard the train as it was just starting out
for memphis. we marched 6 miles when we came to old town creek
where we stoped to rest & eat our dinner when the rest of the
armey came up & the first thing we new the rebs was fireing in our
rear. the cav was then ordered back to the rear where we held the
rebs very easy untill the infantry reinforced us by sending balls out
of our spencers 9 inches apart. we camped

　16: last night we camped on old town creek after giveing the
rebs a good thrashing, driveing them back & killing a great many of
the bloody rascals. we did not have any more battle with them that
night. this morning we started at 4 oc, the 4th in advance of the
train. we marched 13 miles, came to a small town Ellisvill were we
stoped for a while. then we marched 2 miles further & camped. we
had some little skirmishing in the advance & in the rear but not to
amount to anything. we got some prisiners & some horses but they
was gurillies. we sliped up on them

　17: last night about 10 oc Co M & one Co of the 3rd iowa was
ordered out on picket. dismounted, sent our horses back, lay on our

arms all night. their had been a small band of rebs saw cloce their but they did not bother us any all night but one or two shots was fired on another road. the advance started in the morning. at 4 oc had our horses. we was then releaved. marched 10 miles. came to new allbany. their we stoped eat our breakfast & fed our horses. we then went 5 miles further & camped for the night. we was out of rations. had to live off of the country & it was a slim live but we got plenty of potatoes

18: this morning we marched at 5 oc. had to run apast the whole train. stoped at 11 oc, rested, fed our horses, then moved 2 miles further & camped on a very nice streem, tipton creek. we are al out of rations. have to live on potatoes, chicken & fresh pork. we have no more with the train so we have nothing to do but rest

19: marched at 6 oc. came onto salom. say their untill 4 in the eavening when their was a train of 32 wagons came from legrange with rations. we then rec orders to stay all night & eat some so that we could feel like marching. we was a glad set of men. we had plenty of feed for our horses

20: started for legrange at 6 oc. got their at 2 oc, 16 miles. went into camp at Woolf river. drew rations & horse feed, washed off in the river & felt fine. very hot. have not had any bother with rebs for 2 days

21: I rote to louisa, letter No 17. lay in camp all day. some of our sick boys went to camp. brother will [Gantz]* was at legrange

22: started this mor. for memphis. very pleasant all day but very dusty. we marched from legrange to Collarsville, 25 miles, & camped for the night. drew more rations. I rested fine as any one could. had rosten ears for supper & breakfast

THE Fourth Iowa Cavalry, which was part of the reconnoitering force that left Memphis, Tennessee, May 29, 1864, returns after a four-hundred-mile trek.

23: started this morning at sunup & got to memphis at 3 oc, 25 miles. the dust was about 6 inches deep. when I got to camp, I rec 3 letters from lou, but I was so tiered & dirty I could hardely read them

24: letter No. 18. very warm but pleasant. I rote a letter to louisa but was not very well for I had a very bad cold & was sick myself

25: lay around camp. done nothing. got a letter from lou this eave

26: nothing of importance going on. very dry & disty. was rain very bad. I am still unwell

27: in camp winslow near memphis. I was on duty to take a Co. L man to the irving block but he hid & could not be found

28: we are diging a well in the Com. I am not well & I am not doing anything

29: lay in camp this eavening. went on headquarters gard. still very dry & dusty

30: rote to lou, letter No. 19th. done nothing els onley tend to my horse & begin to feel better

31: had sunday morning inspection day. fine weather, cloudy but no rain yet

August 1864

1: some of our boys are on picket today. some working on the well & the rest doing nothing & I am amongest the last. A. Dunns* discharg has come. we had a nice shour of rain last night & is raining by shoures today. this eavening I rec. a letter from lou

2: a scout started out this morning but did not go very far untill they return. I was on stable gard to fateague

3: rote to louise, letter No. 20th. nothing of importence today. we are laying in Camp winslow. I am well & harty

4: the 4th iowa started out on the scout. I went out on picket with 3 men. went on the phinando [Hernando] rod. we got plenty of mellons, aples, peaches, tomates & many other things too tedids to mention. had a good time generaly

5: I was releaved this morning at 8 oc. plenty of mellons & aples to eat. brought 4 in with us. nothing going on at pressent

6: lay in Camp. done nothing

7: rote a letter for how [Howe]* & allso to Geapanrost. nothing going on at present of importence

8: letter no. 21. this was a very nice day. this eave I rote a letter for craff [Craft].* Andrew [Gantz]* got here this eavening from little rock A

9: I went up to the 3rd iowa on a pass to see Andrew.* I stayed their all day. 2 of our men started home on sick furlows, R Kelley [Kelly]* & E. Skers [Skeers]*

10: this day I was down to town on fateague duty. had to load hay & oats all day. I got to see a letter from phlavres remines [?] to stating that he had saw John [Gantz]* on the 9th of July & he was well

11: letter No. 22. lay in camp. 4 of our boys came in off of the scout. said the rest was well. I rote a letter to louisa s. gantz

12: lay in camp. it rained very hard near all day

13: this day I was on camp gard. it raned some

14: this is a very nice day. I rote a letter for how [Howe].* I allso was to church at 2 oc. this eavening 3 of our boys came in reported the Co all rite

15: this is a very nice day. I rote a letter to lou. I allso rote one to Mrs. Craff [Craft].* I was on fateague this eave

16: I was on picket today with 3 men on No 7 pijon roost rod. we had a very good time. got plenty of vegtables & saw plenty of women

17: releaved from picket about 10 oc. worked 2 hours. I rec a letter from lou, No. 20. rained in the afternoon & I slep

18: rained all day. I slept all forenoon on. wasked some this after. I rote a letter for Craft* to the iowa 2nd

19: it rained all night & is raining yet this morning. 5 of our boys came in last night from the reg. the com have left holley springs

20: this morning I went to the 3rd iowa to see Andrew [Gantz]* & the rest of the boys. this afternoon we drew rations

CONFEDERATE General Forrest hadn't given up on Memphis. With two thousand selected men and horses, he arrived successfully. Just before daybreak on August 21, they attacked and were able to get to the heart of the city before the Union forces could be rallied for the defense, according to the regimental history.

21: letter No. 24th. this morning at 3 oc the rebs mad a raid into memphis. at 5 we received orders to sadle & got out to fight.

we then went to the pigon rost road where we run into the rebs.
had a small skirmish. the rebs retreated. we followed after them.
could not cach any of them. we then rturned, went out the
Henando road after the retreating enemy which the rest of the force
had drove out of town. we had some skirmishing in their rear. we
allso sent out a flag of truce & exchanged some sick prisiners the
rebs had taken

22: last night we sent a wagon load of provision to our
prisiners with a flag of truce. we started after the rebs this morning.
found one of our men dead at noon laying by the fence. he had
been marched so hard that he fell over dead. we buried him, then
went on to hernando found a few rebs their but they soon skedaled.
we then came back 12 miles & camped for the night

23: this morning we started at 4. came into camp. got in at 9
nearly give out. after eating our breakfas we had another allarn but
it was fauls

24: lay in camp today & rested for we neaded it for we was
out without rations, blankets anything to rest on or to eat - I rote a
letter for how [Howe]*

25: letter no. 25. Com M was on petroll this morning. started
at 2 oc. went out on the hernando road. I rote to lou & to mother
smith* I allso sent a bulliton home. I was on fateague this afternoon

26: I went out last night with 4 men to visit 4 suspicious
houses & destroy their drink & arrest all men that was their that
had no business their. we went to the places but did not find any
one their so we returned at 11 oc at night

27: lay in camp. done nothing. andrew [Gantz]* was here to
see me. drew rations for 5 days

28: I shaved all my beard of for the first time. I went out to the
3 iowa this afternoon. got some waughter mellon to eat

29: this morning I rote a letter for craff [Craft].* then went on
gard at gard mount. I then rote a letter for Mrs. harris*

30: came off of gard at 8 oc. rote a letter to lou, No. 26. the
boys came in this eavening all rite. did not have much fighting to
do. had been gone 27 days

31: nothing of importence going on. we mustered & had
inspection of arms

September 1864

1: last night I was on petroll. several of the 3rd iowa boys was here & allso several of the 45th iowa. we rec orders for a scout to start this eavening. I loaned Wm. garet 2 dollars

WHEN word was received that Confederate General Price's army of twenty thousand men had reached Lexington, Missouri, and intended to march toward St. Louis, about 525 of the strongest men in the Fourth Iowa Cavalry were ordered to join the campaign to drive the Rebels from Missouri. Gantz was included in this group, which left Memphis, Tennessee, on September 2, 1864, and swung widely into Arkansas—almost to Little Rock—then to Missouri, entering near Poplar Bluff on September 28. The troops advanced almost daily, catching up with Price's force on October 22 at Independence, Missouri, where they fought for two days.

2*: rec letter no. 27. last night at 3 oc we started on a scout. got down to the river in memphis. lay their untill noon, then crossed the river. marched the afternoon. got plenty of watermellon. marched 20 miles

3: marched at 4 oc. crossed blackfish lake at 9 oc. while some of the 1st brigade was crossing the ferey sunk, drownded 3 men & 4 horses. we went 2 miles from their & camped. marched 12 miles

4: marched at 10 oc. crossed st fransis riv. went into camp to wate for the rest of the brig. marched 18 mi

5: marched at 4 oc. crossed the swamp. rained all day prety hard. we marched 40 miles. went into camp after dark, tiered & sleepy

6: marched at 4 oc. got to clarington at 2 oc on white river. mar 20 ms

7: lay here untill noon I rote a letter to lou letter no. 28th today at noon we crossed white river went into camp drew 5 days rations

8: started at 5 oc. crossed a large prairie. saw some gurillies. camped at noon at mans lake. it was a very nice place. we marched 15 miles today. very hot

9: started at 4 oc. got to brownsville station at noon & camped. marched 15 miles. very hot & nasty camping at brownsville. nasty waughter

10: lay here at brownsv station. washed ourselves & clothing. very poor camp in the brush. very hot & swultry

11: letter no. 29th. laying in camp. drew 5 days rations. rote to lou

12: in camp. very hot. we went to graze our horses about one mile. caried some hay in to feed

ARKANSAS

13: very hot

14: lay in camp. done nothing but graised our horses

15: lay in camp at brownsv. I was on detail with 8 men to town, with 8 men after rations for the reg. I rote a letter to lou, letter No. 30th

16: last night I was on stable gard. it was very pleasant today

17: this morning at 6 we started out after forage. got plenty of corn. I rote to lou, No. 31st

18: we left to station. passed through brownville, then went on passed through auston where the 9th iowa was in camp at noon. in the eavening passed through stony point, then went into camp at 9 oc, marched 35 miles

19: marched at 4 oc. did not have any feed for our horses. last night came onto searcy, found some corn fed our horses, then went on through searcy. crossed little read river, then forded at the old fery went into camp. had plenty of corn. marched 25 miles

20: marched at 6 oc. went 20 miles, camped at fairview for the night. Co M & A was on picket. I was on one post with 8 men. we had a very good time on my post. we had all the chickens & tatoes we could eat. we stold the chickens of one women, then borrowed the potatos, coocked them. did not have very much corn

21: marched at 8 oc. came to the river, crossed, went into camp. had plenty of corn. some of us boys washed ourselves & shirts. marched 15 mi

22: last night drew rations. start at 5 oc. passed near sulpher rock. came onto black river & camped. one negrow was shot

axcidently & allso one man of the 19th penn Cav shot himself while
steeling. he tried to open a trunk with his revolver & it went off &
shot him through. marched 20 miles

23: worked all night at a bridge acrost black river. finished it
aganst noon, then crossed. marched 12 miles & camped. we crossed
at elgin. did no have very much for ourselves or horses to eat

24: marched at 3 oc. went 10 miles. stoped got our own
breakfast. fed horses, rested 3 hours then started on the 4th iowa.
left the rest of the command. the 4th went to Powhaten on white
river. Com E went on petrol to smithville. the rest of the reg
camped at powhaten. we marched 25 miles

25: started at 3 oc. got to pocahontes at 10 oc. did not find any
rebs their. went 4 miles further & camped. marched 15 miles today.
had plenty of sweet potatoes & chicken to eat for breakfast

26: started at 5 oc. went 2 miles, crossed blackriver, went 1
mile, counter marched. crossed back at the same place, then marc
12 miles further, makeing 15 miles. got into camp at 9 oc. I had a
chill today & was very near gon up. camped after dark

27: started at 4 oc without our breakfast. went 6 miles, fed, got
something to eat, rested 3 hours. then went 8 miles & camped. very
rainy all day. I feel some better. did not have any chill. I am taking
medison

28: started at 8 oc. did not rain any last but cloudy this
morning. we came 8 miles, crossed black river, then crossed the
arkansas line, got into Mo. then marched 5 miles further. camped
for the night

29: last night it rained all night & is still raining some. we
marched through a very mushy swamp. marched 15 miles &
camped to wate for the infantry & train. I am still geting better. did
not have any chill today

MISSOURI

30: 377 miles this month marched. started at 6 oc. marched 7
miles. came to a town on black river, poplars bluff, Butler Co. left
their at 12. marched 6 miles, camped. was out of rations. rained all
afternoon. crossed black river. camped on the bank. I got lots of
prsimons

October 1864

1: marched at 5 oc. it was raining. onley marched 12 miles &
camped. we got 6 prisoners, some horses, several deserters from
prices armey last night. we drew rations

2: marched at 6 oc. went 5 miles. found that we was on the
rong road. turned to the rite. marched 6 mi. camped at greenville,
Green Co. I lost my pipe. the infantry camped here wit us tonite

3: marched at 4 oc. passed through a little town, hogey, in 3
miles came to castheville. 3 miles further & camped at 12 oc. just at
dark the 4 Mo. started for Jackson Mo. we had plenty to eat of all
kinds of vegetables

4: marched at 2 oc last night. went 20 miles stoped & fed & got
dinner before we started. it rained very hard. marched 12 mi
further & camped at Jackson. it was a very nice little town. it is very
cool this eavening but we are in a good place & have good fiers &
plenty to eat

5: marched at 6 oc. got to Cape Fernardo [Girardeau] at 11.
went into camp. this is a very fine day. some cool after the rain
yesterday. drew 3 days rations. marched 11 miles

6: we are laying in camp at the cape. I went down to town
which was one mile. we are out of mon

7: this morning we came down to the river. got abord of the
boat started for St. Louis, Mo.

8: we are still on the boat. got to St. Louis at 8 oc. went out to
benton barracks. I rote a letter to Louisa, No. 32

9: we was busy all day geting our horses shod. we are now in
benton barracks St. Louis

10: I was on gard over some clothing. drew some clothing this
eave. I rote a letter to lou, No. 33

11: left the barracks at sun up. very warm day. marched 23
miles. camped in 3 miles of manchester

12: marched at 6 oc. very nice rods. we marched 20 miles
today. had plenty of aples to eat & corn for our horses camped in a
very nice place in 2 miles of Washington, Mo. on the Mo. river

13: started at 6 oc. I rec 2 letters from lou. just as we was going
into washington 2 batallions of our reg was taken up to force, the
malitia out in the field. they refused to go but we brought them to

terms. we marched 24 mi & camped. waughter & feed was very
scarce but we got some

14: started at 6 oc. marched 22 miles & camped for the night

15: marched at 6 oc. crossed gasconader, passed through Jule.
marched 18 miles. roads rockey

16: started at 6 oc. marched 15 miles. camped at 4 oc. had to
go 5 miles after corn for our horses. got into a regular catholic town.
very strict

17: started at 4 oc on the callifornia road. passed in 3 miles of
jefferson City. pased risselville. marched 20 miles, went into camp.
drew 5 days rations

18: started at 4 oc. went 9 mi. came to callafornia. marched 12
miles further & camped. march 21 miles. very nice weather

19: started at 5 oc. passed through auterville, then farmer city.
here we saw about 50 young women at a school. they waved their
handkerchiefs for they was glad to see us. then came to sedalia
where we camped. we marched 25 miles. saw the 1st iowa cav here

20: marched at 5 oc. crossed a larg prairie. began to rain this
morning & rained some untill after noon, then began to snow &
snowed is untill after we went into camp which was 9 oc. marched
30 miles

21: last night just after we got into camp their was an order
came in for a detal of 1 corporal & 2 men to report to brigad
headqts. I was detaled. we reported to Col. Winslow.* he had a
dispach he wanted caried to Gen. Pleasinton [Pleasonton].* so I
took the dispach & started. got their just at 2 oc then had to bring 2
more dispaches back from pleasinto to Gens. Smith* and Winslow.
got back just in time to eat breakfast. we came in a very large
orchard, or the rest did, where the ground was covered with aples.
moved out this morning at 5 oc. got to lexington at noon where we
expected to find price* but they had skedadled. we went 5 miles
further & camped. marched 25 miles. I was geting some tiered for I
had been in my sadle for 36 hours & some of this time very cold.
today was pleasant

22: last night we was called out in a hurry at 12 oc. went 8
miles on double quick, then come to a hault. stood in line of batle
untill day, then started on in a fast march. over took prices* rear at
10 oc & have been fighting him ever since. he is on the retreat. they

left 12 of their men dead in one place that I saw. I onley saw one of ours still. after then on the run we passed through independence at 4 oc. the ladies run out & gave us waughter & them that had time some thing to eat. very glad to see us but we did not have onley time to get a drink. had a hard fight here. we are now through the town. the 3 iowa are dismounted, fighting. got some of their men killed & wounded. the 4 iowa dismounted at 8 oc & went into it — marched 25 miles—fought & skirmished 2 hours & the rebs drew off. we then lay in line of battle untill morning then

23: was ordered forward. skirmished 2 miles where we run onto their whole armey in blockade. we then come to a hault untill we was reinforced. then went into it. had some very hard fighting but I saw a great many of the johneys layed out where they would not bother us any more. their was allso some of our men sent to their long homes. but we drove them out of their corks & mad them scud. after we mad that charge, we was releaved. then we got something to eat. marched 2 miles further—for the rest was driveing them —we then stoped & fed our horses. we had not more than fed when the rebs mad their apperance. we bridled & started for them but found they was not going to bother us, so we fed again. our horses did not have more than time to eat when to horse sounded. we mounted & started off on double quick. run 2 miles. saw the rebs. charge was sounded & we charged rite into their lines & they got out of their in a hurry. we then followed them for about 2 miles. then went into camp. had plenty of good waughter & corn for our horses. I rested splended after fighting so hard. marched 15 miles

CONFEDERATE General Price's next stand was twenty miles south of the Missouri River where his remnant force of about ten thousand men met the Union army in full view of each other in the middle of a prairie. The Rebels retreated. The Union army was victorious, but found itself in a mostly desolate country short of supplies in the winter.

24: started at 8 oc. struck a very large prairie. marched hard all day but did not get to overtake any johneys. marched 60 miles but did not stop at dark but went on till 12 oc at night. would not have stoped then if it had not been for runing on the rebs & skirmished with them untill. morning it is raining some

25: this morning just as soon as it got light we advanced on them. had some fighting to do. Co. M went off on the rite & dismounted—I mean the 4th iowa—to fight but the rebs scud & we did not get into it. we was then at the trading post in Kansas. we then mounted & started after them. run them 5 miles & came to where they had taken a stand on a large prairie. we did not halt untill charge was sounded, then fighting commensed but the rebs could not stand our 6 shooters & the part we was fighting could not stand & broke. we captured over one thousand prisners, several officers Gens. Marmaduke,* Cabell* & others. killed a great many. got 7 peaces of artillery & small arms no end. our armey scatered & their armey run in every direction. we then came to a hault to get togeather & the rebs scud. we rested 1 hour, then after them again. charged them 2 more times before night. they run every time but we did not get our reg captured—Kansas—2 reb flags quite so good a thing on them after that but we killed many of them. we allso got a great many of our men killed & wounded. we would have run them further but our horses was so near run down that we had to stop rite out in the prairie for the night. did not have any wood to coock with or anything to ty our horses to but I rested very nice. marched 25 miles & fought all of the time

26: started at 9 oc. went to Ft. Scott, 4 miles. their our brigade stoped & lay all day. Gen. Curtis* moved on after price.* we drew rations, washed, put on some clean clothes. I rote to lou, No. 34

27: started at 8 oc in the rear of the whole armey, 10 miles come to Ft. McKee. then crossed a large prairie. camped at 9 oc at night makeing 38 miles today

28: started at 7 oc, 5 miles, fed our horses. then marched 20 miles further & camped on spring river at sundown

29: started at 7. went 3 miles, fed, got some aples, then mar 12 miles & camped. drew 4 day rations. camped cloce to a very large orchard. had plenty of eatables such as aples, fresh hog, sheep, beef, chickens &c. while James & I was asleep our blankets caught afire. burnt us pretey bad & allso near spoiled Gumms

30: started at 6 oc. at 9 passed through granville. next came to a town newtonia where our advance had a hard fight but they drove the rebs. some of our men was left their. we went 3 miles

further & fed. some of the boys set the prairie on fire. burnt up the
farm & singed & smoked us some—this month we marched 607
miles—we then started on. we then crossed, went on acrossed the
prairie & camped in the age of the timber. marched 25 miles today

31: last Co. M was on picket. the 4th mo. run a mill all night.
we started at 4 oc. got over 80 bushels of meal, but was about out of
breadstuff. we then marched onto cassville. their was some more of
our troops. we stoped their one hour. then started out south.
passed through keethville, 8 miles & camped. very rough country.
all the buildings was burnt. the 1st plattoon went after corn—
marched 25 miles today—we had to run our horses 3 miles before
we got any corn

November 1864

1: started at 8 oc. Gen. Curtis* passed us this morning. we
onley marched 5 miles & camped. it began to rain & rained all day

2: did not move camp today. squad 5 fixed up a tent out of
their guns. rained all day. I went after corn. I rote a letter to lou, No.
35

3: it snowed last night & is snowing this morning. marched at
9 oc. passed through the pearidy batle field. marched 20 miles. still
snowing. camped in the woods

4: last night we camped near cross hollows. moved at 5 oc.
cold & snowing. we onley marched 15 miles. came to fayettville
where price* had been fighting with a small force of our men. the
1st ark was their & some molitia, about 12 hundred in all. when
price* found we was comeing, he scud. we camped for the night at
fayettville

5: I rote a letter to louisa, No. 36. we moved from here at 1 oc.
marched 10 miles, camped at prairie grove. had plenty of corn for
our horses. allso plenty of aples to eat

6: very windy all night. marched at 6 oc. passed corn hill &
boonsville, then camped on illinois river in the indian nation.
marched 20 miles. did not have any rations or any feed for our

horses

7: marched at 7 oc. we are now in the indian nation. their is nothing in this part of the country for the rebs drove the indians away. marched 30 miles. did not camp untill 11 oc at night. then did not have anything for ourselves or horses to eat. prety col tonight

8: marched at 7 oc. was raining some. went to the arkansas river at rebel falls between fort smith & Ft. Gibson. did not find any rebs but plenty of trash such as dead horses, old wagons &c. we then came back 2 mi & went into camp. did not have anything to eat but beef. still raining. today was lexion day but no vote

9: last night it rained very hard. marched at 8 oc. several of our boys had to pool it. I was dismounted. marched 15 miles. camped had nothing to eat but meet

10: started at 5 oc. horses near all gave out. the most of the boys have to walk. we got plenty of corn for our horses. boiled & grited some for cakes. out of rations. had plenty of beef. marched 20 miles. camped on a very nice streem

11: started at 6 oc. marched very slow. our horses was near played. I was dismounted. camped before night on a nice streem. had plenty of beef & chicken to eat. marched 15 miles. our forager came in after night. had plenty of meal, so we got at it & had a big super

12: started at 3. passed through cainhill & boonsville. came on to prairie grove & camped. marched only 15 miles. Com M went on picket. some bushwhackers here. we had some men killed by them. our foragers came in with plenty of everything that was good to eat. then their was 18 wagons came from fayattvill with rations. we lived fat. had plenty aples & fresh meet of all kinds. allmost foundered

13: started at 7 though some very hilley country. marched 15 miles. very prety day. had plenty of corn for horses

14: marched at 6 oc. I went on ahead & led my horse. I got plenty of molasses. had slapjacks & lasses for supper. marched 20 miles

15: looked some like rain. marched at 6 oc. had plenty to eat. marched 25 miles. camped cloce to cassville. drew 4 days rations

16: some cloudy & misty. I turned over my horse. picked up

another. started this morning at 8 oc. passed through cassville. marched 25 miles. did not rain any. cleared of & is a very nice day. had plenty corn

17: started at 6 oc. very pleasant phorenoon. this afternoon it began to rain & rained untill near mid night. marched 25 miles. camped at a little town, little york. in 10 miles of springfield, mo. it was about 8 at night. had plenty of corn

18: marched at 6 oc. got to springfield at noon. went into camp. it is clear but cool. marched 10 miles

19: laying here in camp resting. I was on gard. we drew rations & clothing

20: rote to lou, No. 37. lay in camp. done nothing but make fires for it was very cold & snowing some but we are enjoying it well

21: still in camp at springfield. I was on duty getting the horses shod. very cold & spiting snow this eavening

22: left springfield at 6 oc. very cold & snowing. cold all day. camped before sun down. had plenty of corn & hay & a good place to camp. marched 25 miles

23: started at 6 oc. pleasanter then it was yesterday. camped at lebanon. did not have any corn for our horses. marched 25 miles

24: marched at 4 oc. had to march prety fast on the account of geting to where their was waughter & feed for our horses. marched 32 miles. camped at wainesville. had plenty of corn for our horses for we made a rade on the quartermaster at wainesville & took all his corn. had a very good camp. plenty of wood. cool tonight

25: marched at 6 oc. I started a head. walked 12 miles to big piney. I then got on my horse. rode 8 miles to little piney. their we camped before night. marched 20 miles. in a very good camp. had plenty of oats for horses

26: started at 6 oc. got to rolleigh at noon. saw closs & clint campbell. turned over our horses, 17 of them. got on the carrs at 9 oc. started for st. louis. roll. is a very hard place. rained some this afternoon

FROM the time it left Memphis, Tennessee, in September until it returned to St. Louis, Missouri, in November, the Fourth Cavalry had logged 1,952 miles, worn out two sets of horses, and suffered extreme heat, cold, and lack

of provisions, the regimental history reported. Many of the men were discharged for disabilities brought on as much by the conditions as the enemy.

27: got to st. louis at 4 oc this morning. all the boys went out to benton barrack but me & my mess. we garded the sadles & other things untill they could send a wagon

28: at the depo yet on gard. they did not send any wagons last night. the wagons came at 3 oc so I put the things on & went out to the barracks. I then rote a letter to louisa, No. 38th

29: nothing of importence

30: at benton barracks

December 1864

1: rec 9 leters from home. 5 from other places. I rote one to lou, No. 39

2: lay in camp at the barrack. this brigade made a rad on the bake shop at st. louis. got 1400 loaves

3: nothing of importance

4: had inspection for the purpose of finding some man that had dirdered [murdered] a citizen but did not find him

5: I went down to the christion commish. rote No. 40

6: done nothing

7: rote a letter to lou, No 41st

8: at the barracks. very cool weather

THE portion of the Fourth Iowa Cavalry, including Gantz, which had gone to battle Price in Missouri and Kansas, left St. Louis bound for Louisville, Kentucky. There it met up with the remainder of the companies that had stayed in the Memphis, Tennessee, area.

9: embarked abord the steamer St. Patric at St Louis

10: on the river, going down the river big mardy

11: land at cairo about 3 oc but did not get off the bot

12: lay at cairo on the st. patric. I rote a letter to lou, letter No.

42nd

 13: on the st. patric at cairo. weather pleasant. I rote to lou, No. 43

 14: still out the boat at cairo

 15: today we moved off of the boat. went into barracks at cairo. I rote to lou, No. 44th. I was on gard on the boat to keep citizens off

 16: lay in barracks at cairo. raining some. I rote a letter to, lou No. 45th

 17: got abord of the st. patric bound for louisville but it was so fogy that the boat could not run. we was crowded some

 18: we onley run about 1 mile. lay on the boat just above cairo. very fogy

 19: started this morning but it as so fogy that we did not run far

 20: we are now mooveing at a very good rate. the Ohio river is very nice

 21: run all night at a good rate. we are now between [blur] & Ky. was stoped at evinsville to load on some forage. I rote a letter to lou, No. 46

 22: run all night this morning. came to town where their was some guerillies on the ky side. had fired into some of the troops before us. we saw them but they did not fire into us. we wanted to go for them but cap would not let us. they did not fire into us or we would have went any how for we was read for them

 23: we landed at louisville about dark. came through the town. went into camp. did not have any wood or tents. very cold. we near froze. get into camp at 10 oc. carried rails. got some supper. layed down about 12 oc with a big fire

 24: we are now laying in camp at louisville. we are haveing very hard times. have no tents or barracks & it is very cold

 25: nothing of importence. No money & christmas but we rec mail. I got one letter which was a treet to me

 26: nothing going on. still in camp at louisville. I rote to lou, No. 47th

 27: in camp. weather more pleasant

 28: very cold & windy. still in camp at louisville. we rec pay. I drew 156 dollars

29: moved camp this morning. I bought some lumber. we put up a shebang. I was on fateague duty

30: got some more lumber. enlarged our shebang. made bunk, fixed some other things & c.& c

31: I went to town & got a cook stove & riged our shebang in good order & built a good fire in it & I felt so well I did not know what to do for the day was cold & snowing some—so ended the year A.D. 1864 I will now begin a new book & lay this away for safe keeping—J. S. Gantz

1865

January 1865

1*: I am in camp. brother will [Gantz]* is here with me all day. it is very cool. we kept good fires & set by them & rote letters, eat aples, & c. I rote to lou, N 1st

2: lay in camp at louis. more moderate today

3: the boys came from memphis, the concale. very cool this eavening

4: still in camp. some stormey

5: in camp doing very well. raining some

6: in camp at louisvile. I was on gard at head quarters. very cold

7: it began to rain this morning. rained all day. very disagreeable

8: last night it snow all night & is snowing today. very nasty

9: this morning clear. James & I went to town got our pictures taken. I rote to lou, No. 2nd

10: very nice day. not quite so disagreed. nothing of importence

11: not of importence. rote a letter to lou, No 3

12: sittng in camp. don nothing

13: thawing & misting some. eck & I was to town got some

pictures

14: I was on gard last night. very nice day

15: I lay in camp all day & rote near all the time. cool & some cloudy

16: some of our boys come up. weather cool & some cloudy all day. laying at louisville

17: very cool. the rest of the boys came up from below. had a kind of crowded time

BY now, the entire regiment was reassembled and a strong cavalry corps was organized to sweep over the portion of the South where the remaining Rebel forces were concentrated. This would be the final struggle of the war in this theater.

18: cool but very pleasant. I am siting by the stove. I rec. a letter form louisa. I allso rote one in answer, No. 4

19: this morning it began to snow. snowed prety fast until 10 oc. I was on camp gard. very prety afternoon

20: off gard this morning. went to town. got an album. we drilled this afternoon

21: Louisville. raining some this morning. rained all day. I did nothing but set in the tent. drew rations

22: lay in camp at louisville. very pleasant. I rote a letter to lou, letter No. 5. I also rec one from lou

23: snowed very hard all night & is still snowing this morning. I went to town this afternoon. the tenth Mo. got abord of the boat to leave this place. I suppose for east port allabama

24: KY. very cold this morning. spiting snow some. I went over to the 3rd Iowa to see will [Gantz]*

25: this morning was very cold. I went to the [crossed out] on gard, on gard at headquarters. I then rote a letter to lou, No. 6th

26: it is colder this morning than it has been this winter. Wm. Lee* & I went to town this fore noon. Wm Smith* [crossed out] got drunk. E Co. of the 3rd iowa start this eavening

27: KY. nothing of importence going. on I rec a letter from lou. it is a very cold day

28: very cold today. I went to town. got an album

29: this is a very prety day. we had inspection. I rec 3 letters

from home & one from E.G.D. [Dearduff]* I allso rote a letter to lou,
No. 7th

    30: more pleasant today than common. we drilled this
afternon. I rote a letter to E.G. Dearduff*

    31: KY. very warm & pleasant. looks some like rain. we are
drilling this after noon. I rote a letter to Ettie. nothing of importence

February 1865

    1: nothing of importence. we are in camp at louisville

    2: it rained all day. it was very mudy. I was on gard to night
the reg. presented a sabor to Col. Winslow*

    3: still warm & pleasant & allso very mudy

    4: all things quiet. very mudy. still in camp at louisville, ky.
No. 8th [letter]

    5: very cool last night. very nice & pleasant today. I rote a
letter to lou. we had inspection

    6: very pleasant. I expressed a lot of things home today. allso
loaned a lot of money. Mr. vance* started home. part of this brig got
on the boats

THE *regiment had been ordered to Eastport, Mississippi, but Gantz's
company actually exited the boat in Waterloo, Alabama. From there, they
marched through the hilly northwestern portion of Alabama for what would
be the last push of the Union forces—and certainly the last for Gantz—on the
western front.*

    7: this morning we came down to the river. got on the boat
nora about noon. I run all over town. we did not leave louisville
untill after night. on river letter No. 9.

    8: last night we started from louisville at dark. run over the
rapids very rough. run aganst the bank. made the boat leak. we had
to lay up 2 or 3 hours we the started. run all night. it is very cold.
snowed some all day today. my eyes are very sore but are getting
better. I rot a letter to lou

9*: very cold last nite. we run all night. my eyes hurtin very much, so much that I did not sleep any. the ice was very bad on river tenn.

10: I lay in bed all day with the sore eyes. got to paduca at 11. took the horses of. cleaned off the boat. put the horses on & loaded some coal. I was so blind I did not see piduce at all

11: last we left pidca just after dark with a very larg fleet, looked very nice for the was tied 2&2 togeather through the hole fleet. my eyes are better today so that I can see some

ALABAMA

12: very pleasant. we are on the tenn. river. got to east port at 4 oc, then went up the river 3 miles. landed on the alla. shore at waterloo but did not get off of the boat. my eyes was very sore

13: very cool this morning. got off the boat. started for camp, 13 miles. I saw some of the 8th iowa cav. boys lot out to camp before night. I went & eat supper with brother will*

GRAVILLE SPRINGS, ALABAMA

14: lay in camp all day. done nothing. my eyes hurt me so that I could not get out of the house

15*: rained some last night & is still raining some today. I do not dare go out any. my eyes are so sore. bad luck

16: this is a very bleasat morning. my eyes are some better. this afternoon we moved our shanty up to the Co. seveal of the boys of Co. M have the sore eyes. one man of Co H died today

17: we are working on our shebang. this is a very nice day

18: warm & pleasant. we have a very nice camp. me eyes are better

19: very nice day. we had inspection this morning at 9. we allso had dress perade this eavening at 5

20: warm & pleasant. non commish drilled 2 today. not of

importence going on. we are at gravely springs alla in barracks of our build. letter No. 10

21: some cloudy. looks very much like rain. very winday. I rote a letter to louisa S. Gantz

22: it rained last nite near all night & is raining all day today. we lay in camp. got some mail this eavening. I got one letter from lou

23: still raining all day. 12 of Co H has the small pox

24: it is not raining but is still very cloudy. we are going to work at stables. it is very mudy. letter No. 11

25: last night it rained all night & untill noon today then it cleared off—I rec a letter from lou—very nice. I was on stable gard today. have a very bad cold

26: very nice day. had inspection of horses & quarters. allso received orders to get horses shod. I rote a letter to lou

27: very pleasant. we had Gen. inspection in the afternoon. in the eavening sprinkeled some

28: did not rain any last night. mustered for pay. drilled this afternoon. James Taylor* got back to the co. today

March 1865

1: very pleasant morning. I rec. a letter from lou. we drilled this morning on foot. this afternoon mounted. boxed our things today to send home. clouded up this eavening. rained some. their was a scout started out of the 4th iowa this eavening, small squad from Co M. letter No. 12

2: last night it raned all night & all day today. I rote to lou

3: still raining. very wet. rained all day. we are not doing anything. still at gravely springs Alla

4: rained near all night. last night has some appeerence of clearing of today. very mudy

5: this is a very beautiful morning. after the rain we had sunday morning inspection. I rec a letter from lou. I was on stable gard this eavening. letter No. 13

6: this is a very nice day. we drilled this afternoon. I rote a letter to lou. the scout came in today

7: warm & pleasant. drilled this forenoon. had grand review this afternoon by Gen. Wilson* I rote a letter to Miss Rebeca Patent

8: rained today. was very disagreeable

9: still raining. some very mudy. cleared off this afternoon. it very cool

10: very cool today & raining some. I was on fateague today to did a sink

11: this is a very nice morning. we had inspection. began this morning at 9 oc & lasted untill 1 oc in the afternoon

12: very pleasant morning. had inspection at 9 oc. the rest of the day nothing to do. I rote a letter to louisa letter, No. 14th

13: very nice day. we drilled twice. I was on stable gard. I rec a letter from lou

14: it rained some last night & is raining yet. we are sending our clothing off. have orders to march soon

15: very pleasant this morning. very hot through the day. I rec a letter from lou. we drilled this afternoon still in camp at gravely springs. I rote a letter to lou to night, letter No. 15th

16: last night it rained very hard. it was still raining this morning when we got up, that was 3 oc when revalee sounded. we left our camp at 6 oc. got waterloo landing at 2 oc in the afternoon. stoped, got something to eat & fed our horses. Just at dark, we mounted, went to the river, got on the boat, crossed the river. came 4 miles, went into camp. got lost several time before we got their, got in at 12 oc at night on a very high hill near east port

17: lay in camp all day, very nice day. I went to see the 8th iowa. found several of the boys that I was acquainted with

18: very pleasant day. we drew some rations & a lot of sanitaries. we are now camped in Miss near east port on a very high hill. have a very good camt

19: very warm. had inspection. drilled some. fixed this afternoon to march. I rote a letter to louisa s Gantz, letter No. 16th

20: very pleasant. we had orders to start this morning at 2 oc but the order was countermanded & we did not go. we are in camp yet

21: I was on stable gard last night. it rained all night & has very near cleared off. we rec orders at 10 oc to be ready to march at 2 oc. I rote a letter & sent it to lou by [John] kelley [Kelly].* we moved at 2 oc, marched 5 miles & camped for the night at 8 oc. very nice camp. slept well

22: very pleasant. we moved at 4 oc. had some very mudy roads. passed some very nice farms, large orchards, the peach trees was out in full bloom. we marched a south east direction. stoped at 2 oc at a very large plantation. got all the chicken & flour & meal we could eat. allso got plenty of corn for our horses. we then marched 5 miles—in all marched 20 miles today—further & camped for the night by the side of a very nice little stream. had plenty of chicken & gravy for supper. got into camp at 5 oc. good time

23: very fine morning. had slapjacks for breakfast. marched at 6 oc, Co M in the rear of the reg. very rough, hilley country & allso some very nice streams made by springs. passed through a part of the country where near all the timber was cedar. their was some rebs in our advance, about one hundred, fired into our advance. we camped at 5 oc on a very good farm but very rockey. had plenty to eat & good waughter, plenty corn for our horses. marched 25 miles

24: marched this morning at 10 oc in the rear of the 2nd brigade. some rebs fired on our advance. 2nd brig went on a road to the left & we to the rite. very fine morning. roads very hilley & rough. we are now carelled on top of a very high hill. we passed through a little town this morning, newbourn. we crossed a very nice stream this eavening by the name of Sypsey, a splendid mill stream, 10 feet of a fall, where we crossed & a mill by the name of gerds mill. camped at 5 oc on a high hill. march 20 miles today. Alla, Walker Co

25: started this morning at 6 oc. very cool last night. very heavy frost. we marched over a very rough hilley & mountaineous country timbered with pine. we did not pas any house all day onley earley this morning. did not get any forage for our horses this night for our horses. marched 30 miles. camped on a very beautiful stream Clear Creek some call it & some black wauter. Alla, Walker Co

26: very pleasant. revalee sounded at 4 oc. did not have anything for breakfast but hardtack & coffey. marched this morning at 7 oc over some more very mountaineous country. we came to 2 or 3 farms at noon. stoped & fed our horses & got something to eat for ourselves. the folks seamed very glad to see us but I know they was glad to see us leave. we stoped again at 3. rested, fed, caried 2 feds with us. crossed black waughter river after dark. very swift current. camped at night at 9 oc with the other brigade. marched 25 miles

27: very pleasant. some cloudy. we are laying in camp wating. we have to build a bridge before we can go any further. the name of the stream is big warrior. the 2nd plattoon has gone after forage. they have found a ford & are fording the river but it is a very nasty ford. lots of the horses falls & floats down the river & some drowns. this afternoon the 1st plattoon went after forage. got plenty. got back & crossed the river just at dark. went into camp. it was raining. we got supper & I went fixed shebangs. got to bed at 9 oc. raining very stirdy

28: last night after we had gone to bed, boots & sadles sounded & we had to get up & march. went rough at the start. we marched 15 miles. came to little warior at 4 oc in the morning. layed their till 12 oc, then we crossed the river & marched 20 miles over some prety rough country. got to a very large plantation, had 200 darkies on it. it was in joneses valley. the planters name is lilley hawkins. we got in here at 9 oc last night. camped in a orchard of the very nicest peach trees. we was very sleepy & tiered. had a very good supper & went to bed slept fine

29: we are in camp yet. prospect to stay here to day. some cloudy, looks like rain. started from this place at 11 oc. passed some very large iron works on the iron mountain rr. marched 17 miles. had some skirmishing with the rebs. got to catauby river after dark. it was so high that we could not cross so we went into camp on a very large hill side. rained all night very hard. some of the boys got wet

30: this morning did not start untill 9 oc. then we crossed on the rail road bridge. after the command got acrossed we started on through dixie. our batallion went one road, Co M in the advance. we passed through Elliottville. run on some pickets. had some skirmishing with them. the 2nd batallion was on the other road. they & we both skirmished all the way till we got to montevallo

where we charged on about 8 hundred. they scud. the force went
into camp. Com M went on picket. we marched 15 miles. very cool
& rained some

    31: we are at montevallo yet & not likely to leave. I am on
gard over a large lot of rebs comisaries such as hardtack, meet, salt,
flour, meal, salt & many other things too tedious to mention at the
RR station. they are now issueing it to the command. [writing goes
from pen to pencil] about 11 oc we was attacted on. the pickets
posts had to fight very hard to keep back the enemy untill we was
reinforced [blur] them back several miles. that night about 4 oc had
a very hard fight. then I was wounded

April 1865

    1[in ink]*: [in pencil] last night about 9 oc we stoped at a house
at plantersville where we [Abbey, O. Chester, Lathers, Riley]*
wounded stayed all night. we see a pretty hard time. this morning
the doc told me that my arm would have to come off & at 7 oc they
amputated my arm which was hard for me but such are the trials of
war. then we was loaded in the ambulances, hauled 5 miles, then
put in a church to stay untill they could send for us & the command
went on for Selma Alla which was 21 miles. left us alone

    1: [this is what he says] our force came on to Selme. charged
into the had some pretty hard fighting but got posesion of selma.
burnt the government works. got plany of stores. all this time I was
laying in the church on my back

*TOWARD the last of April, the remaining men in the Fourth Iowa Cavalry
moved from Alabama and went into camp at Atlanta, Georgia, on May 9,
1865, as the war was ·over. They remained there until August—mainly
patrolling to preserve order—until they were mustered out in August.*

III

After the War

Headquarters First Brigade,
Fourth Division, Cavalry Corps, M.D.M.
Atlanta, Ga., August 7, 1865

General Orders
No. 3

Comrades: The war is ended. The last order you obey directs your return to your homes. Let your future be as commendable as your past has been glorious. Your career as soldiers is over. You go home as citizens, to reap the reward of your campaigns. Your country will always cherish the memory of her brave defenders.

Seven states have been traversed by your columns. Their soil has been consecrated by the blood of your companions. Your victories will impress their localities on your minds. Though the battles of the war are over, let us recollect that those of our lives continue to the end, that our orders are from Him whose plans are always successful, and that justice is no less a divine attribute than mercy. I shall hear of your behavior in civil life, and believe that you will daily evidence the fact that well disciplined soldiers can become equally good citizens. During the long period in which I have been associated with you, I have had many occasions to be proud of your conduct, and have often rejoiced that I commanded such brave men.

While I regret to separate from such gallant officers and men, I rejoice with you that our country is intact and united, our government stronger than ever, and that the necessity for our armed service no longer exists. Confident that, when again required, you will be as ready to take the carbine and saber as you now are to abandon them. I part from you with many and sincere wishes for your future prosperity and happiness.

E. F. Winslow,
Brevet Brigadier General

This farewell order was read by Winslow at a parade of the regiment in Atlanta, Georgia, a few days before the men were mustered out of the Union service on August 10, 1865.[1]

In its four years of existence, the Fourth Iowa Cavalry's roster included 1,952 men. The summary of casualties show 44 killed and 11 who died later of wounds, 120 wounded, and 199 who died of disease. More than 270 were discharged for wounds, diseases, or other causes, 97 were buried in national cemeteries, 94 were captured, and 35 were transferred.[2]

Of the nine Iowa cavalry regiments, the Fourth ranked in the middle in terms of losses. The Fourth Iowa Cavalry's fifty-five men killed in battle—which included four officers and fifty-one enlisted men—lost less than the First, Second, Third, and Fifth but more than the Sixth, Seventh, Eighth, and Ninth.[3]

Jacob Gantz's wound was severe. He had been engaging the Rebels dismounted near Montevallo, Alabama, when a miniball struck him just below the right elbow, fracturing both the humerus and the ulna.[4]

After his arm was amputated about halfway above the elbow, apparently at a house in Plantersville, Alabama, he and the other wounded were transported by ambulances to a church and left alone until further treatment could be arranged. The first note of hospital care in his medical records from the National Archives indicates that Gantz was admitted to Kennedy U.S.A. General Hospital in Mobile, Alabama, on May 5, 1865. He was put aboard the U.S.A. hospital steamer *D.A. January* on May 8, the records reveal, and arrived at U.S.A. General Hospital in Mound City, Illinois, on May 25. After about three weeks in Illinois, Gantz was transported via the U.S.A. hospital steamer *Ginnie Hopkins* on June 14 to the U.S.A. General Hospital in Keokuk, Iowa, where he was admitted on June 18, 1865.

About a month later, 1st Lt. Daniel Vance* signed a certificate requesting a disability discharge for Gantz by describing the seriousness of his wound and adding "in all things he has been a good soldier." The discharge was granted on August 22, 1865.[5]

When Winslow addressed the last of this regiment in Atlanta, Georgia, Gantz was in Iowa continuing to recover from his wound. But the Iowa general's words, his call for the soldiers to make the "future as commendable as your past has been glorious," nevertheless were heeded by Company M's 3d corporal.

Almost five months passed as Gantz made the long trip back to Iowa and good health. As his journals show, he was a strong man of great self-discipline. He had fine-tuned his organizational skills and had no time to mope about his loss of an arm.

Farming at the home place near Brookville was no longer an

option as producers then had to handle powerful teams of horses to till the soil. Although this had been his sole occupation, Gantz quickly moved his family—Louisa, Byron Noble, who was now about four years old, and daughter Minnie Estelle, who was conceived while Gantz was on furlough and born December 1, 1864—to Fairfield, some five miles southeast of Brookville.

Gantz then ran a successful campaign on the Republican ticket for sheriff of Jefferson County, a position he held for six years until 1872.[6] During that time, a third child, Earnest Clyde, was born on May 20, 1868. Myrtle, born on February 2, 1872, at the end of his final term as sheriff, died as a toddler on December 7, 1874.[7]

By this time, Fairfield was a bustling community. In the centennial year of 1876, total business in Fairfield was about $3 million annually, about thirty times as much as it had been in 1847.

Practically every kind of department and specialty store considered a must in modern-day cities existed in Fairfield after the war. There also were agriculture-related industries and factories, cultural endeavors such as an opera house and a large public library, and as many churches as saloons. Four private schools and a college met educational needs in addition to the public school system, and communication was served by three newspapers and three telegraph offices.[8]

Gantz joined the business community in 1872 by opening a boarding facility, The Gantz House, at what is now the corner of North 3rd Street and West Briggs.[9] He had a livery stable in conjunction with the boardinghouse. "Call and see us before you hire or feed your teams or feed yourselves, and see how nicely we can accommodate you. J. S. Gantz" read his advertisements in the *Daily Journal* newspaper. The house was a large, three-story structure with several fireplaces and a balcony porch on the second floor.

He also served one term as tax assessor in Fairfield and owned a 160-acre farm in Black Hawk Township north of Fairfield. Although he had been raised a Baptist, Gantz became an active member of the Methodist Church in Fairfield. He was a leader in the Odd Fellows for thirty-four years and was an honored member of the Grand Army of the Republic (GAR) in which he served as commander in 1890. He also was a delegate to the GAR national encampment in 1885 and attended every national encampment until 1920.[10]

By 1880 three more children had been born to Jacob and Louisa: Grace Leota on December 14, 1875; Albert on July 28, 1878, who died about eighteen months later on November 24, 1879; and James Garfield

Minnie Estelle Gantz, Byron Noble Gantz, and Earnest Gantz,
Fairfield, Iowa.

The Gantz House, Fairfield, Iowa. Jacob Gantz is the fourth adult from the right.

on February 8, 1880. Five children were living—from four months to about twenty years of age—when Louisa became ill and died on June 4, 1880, of pneumonia.[11]

Two years later on November 28, 1882, the forty-seven-year-old Gantz married Margaret Vance Rock, a widow who attended the same church.[12] Thus continued his life and business until the turn of the century.

His daughter Grace L. died in 1906. Byron became a doctor, married, and practiced in Fairfield. Minnie E. became a teacher and moved first to Nebraska and then to California with her husband, Simon Peter Anderson.[13] Their son, Joseph D. Anderson, was the father of Jacqueline Anderson Harris, my mother. No information was located on the occupations pursued by Earnest C. or James G.

In 1912, Gantz agreed to sell the boardinghouse and property to the Board of Education for $5,000 to make room for construction of a high school.[14] At the age of seventy-seven, Gantz, who lived adjacent to the boardinghouse to the north, was beginning to slow down—to relax for perhaps the first time since his youth.

On February 19, 1922, eighty-seven-year-old Jacob S. Gantz died after an illness of several weeks. The Fairfield *Ledger-Journal* carried his obituary on the front page recounting his stint in the Fourth Iowa Cavalry and his community involvement before and after the Civil War. The flag on the courthouse lawn flew at half-mast for Gantz on the day of his funeral February 21, 1922, as the newspaper said, "it has become a beautiful custom to fly the flag at half mast here when one of its defenders goes."[15]

Jacob S. Gantz,
December 25, 1896, Fairfield, Iowa.

APPENDIX

People in the Diaries

THE DIARIES of Jacob Gantz mention numerous comrades, visitors, and relatives, many of whom have been traced and researched in order to provide the reader with more information. They are presented in the following alphabetical listing. The date at the conclusion of each descriptive paragraph notes when Gantz mentioned the person in his diary.

Abbey, Villeroy: A private who was wounded with Jacob Gantz at Six-Mile Creek, Alabama, on March 31, 1865. A native of New York, Abbey was a resident of Worth County when he enlisted in Company M of the Fourth Iowa Cavalry at the age of twenty-five on December 30, 1863. He was mustered out on August 8, 1865, in Atlanta, Georgia. (4-1-1865)

Barnes, Samuel: A native of Ohio, Samuel was living in Fairfield when he enlisted in Company M, Fourth Iowa Cavalry on November 27, 1861, at the age of 31. He was mustered out on December 5, 1864, at Memphis, Tennessee at the conclusion of his term of service. (8-11-1863)

Beall, James M.: Born in Virginia but a resident of Libertyville, Beall, age twenty-seven, joined Company M of the Fourth Iowa Cavalry on November 5, 1861. He was discharged for disability on March 19, 1863, in Helena, Arkansas. (8-21-1863)

Byers, John Y.: This Ohio native and resident of Libertyville joined the Fourth Iowa Cavalry, Company M, on December 14, 1861, at the age of twenty. He reenlisted on December 20, 1863, and was promoted to 4th corporal on January 1, 1865. He was mustered out on August 8, 1865, from Atlanta, Georgia. (12-21-1863)

Cabell, Confederate Gen. William Lewis: Born January 1, 1827, in Danville, Virginia, he was a West Point graduate and had been in the U.S. Regular Army as quartermaster until his resignation in the spring of 1861 to assume that position in the Confederate army. He was captured in Missouri in 1864 and was held at the prisoner of war camp in Fort Warren at Boston, Massachusetts. After the war he became a lawyer and moved to Dallas, Texas, where he died in February 1916. (10-25-1864)

Carson, William: Born in Ohio and living at Fairfield, Iowa, when the war broke out, this twenty-five-year-old enlisted on January 4, 1864. He also did service in the Nineteenth Infantry, Company D, and was mustered out on August 8, 1865, in Atlanta, Georgia. (2-11-1864)

Chester, Lemon: This nineteen-year-old Indiana native and resident of Salina enlisted on October 22, 1861, and was mustered out at Memphis, Tennessee, on December 5, 1864, upon the expiration of his term of service. (10-5-1863, 12-2-1863, 12-3-1863)

Chester, Oliver F.: Chester, a private, was wounded with Jacob Gantz at Six-Mile Creek, Alabama, on March 31, 1865. He was eighteen, a native of Indiana, and a resident of Jefferson County when he joined the Fourth Iowa Cavalry, Company M, on March 21, 1864. He was mustered out at Atlanta, Georgia, on August 8, 1865. (4-1-1865)

Craft, Michael: From his native Germany to his residence in Lockridge, Craft, age twenty-six, decided to join the Union cause on November 25, 1861, when he enlisted in the Fourth Iowa Cavalry, Company M. At the expiration of his term of service on December 5, 1864, he was mustered out at Memphis, Tennessee. (3-22-1863, 4-13-1863, 4-24-1863, 8-8-1864, 8-15-1864, 8-18-1864, 8-29-1864)

Curtis, Gen. Samuel Ryan: Born in Clinton, New York, in 1805, Curtis was an army veteran who resigned his seat as an Iowa congressman to go back to the army as a colonel in 1861. He became U.S. peace commissioner in 1865 and was a Union Pacific Railroad commissioner until eight months before his death in Iowa on December 26, 1866. (10-26-1864, 11-1-1864)

Dearduff, Eli G.: Jacob Gantz's brother-in-law was thirty-two when he enlisted on November 12, 1861, in Company M of the Fourth Iowa Cavalry. He was a resident of Brookville and a native of Ohio who obtained the rank of 3d sergeant on January 1, 1863. He was mustered out at Memphis, Tennessee, on December 5, 1864, upon the completion of his term of service. (3-13-1863, 8-8-1863, 9-6-1863, 10-10-1863, 10-15-1863, 1-29-1865, 1-30-1865)

Dearduff, Martha J.: She was the eldest child of John and Mahala Gantz, sister of Jacob Gantz, and the wife of Eli G. Dearduff. (6-13-1864)

Dunn, Andrew: He was discharged for disability on July 23, 1864, from Memphis, Tennessee. Dunn enlisted at twenty-nine years of age on November 2, 1861. He was a resident of Libertyville and a native of Ohio. (10-31-1863, 12-2-1863, 12-3-1863, 8-1-1864)

Ennis, Joseph: Jacob Gantz's brother-in-law was twenty-six when he enlisted from his home in Brookville on November 2, 1861. A native of Indiana, Ennis was promoted to regimental farrier from farrier of Company D on November 15, 1862. He was mustered out on July 4, 1863. (3-13-1863, 4-12-1863)

Forrest, Confederate Gen. Nathan B.: This southerner worked his way up from a background of little formal education and work as a blacksmith and farmer to one of the most brilliant leaders on either side of the Civil War. Although he led the controversial attack on Fort Pillow, Tennessee, one of Forrest's major victories was at Brice's Cross Roads, Mississippi, where he drove the Union army twice the size of his into retreat and captured a large stash of Union equipment. His last action was in Selma, Alabama, in April 1865. This was during the battles where Gantz was shot. He died in 1877. (June-July 1964 editor's notes)

Gantz, Andrew: Jacob Gantz's brother was twenty-eight when he enlisted in the Fourth Iowa Cavalry, Company F. He was a native of Pennsylvania and a resident of Brookville when he enlisted. He was promoted teamster on October 3, 1862, and was mustered out on September 19, 1864, at the expiration of his term of service. (3-24-1863, 8-8-1864, 8-9-1864, 8-20-1864, 8-27-1864)

Gantz, John Tipten: Jacob Gantz's youngest brother, enlisted on February 11, 1864, at the age of twenty-one and served in the Third Iowa Cavalry. (8-10-1864)

Gantz, Louisa S.: This was Jacob Gantz's first wife. They married in Jefferson County, Iowa, on December 1, 1859, and she had seven children. She died in 1881 at age forty. Jacob wrote many letters to his wife and kept a record of their correspondence throughout his diaries.

Gantz, William: This brother of Jacob Gantz was twenty-three when he enlisted on November 1, 1861, in the Fourth Iowa Cavalry, Company F. He was a resident of Fairfield and a native of Ohio who made 4th corporal on March 1, 1865. Within a month (March 31), he was wounded at Montevallo, Alabama, and was mustered out on August 8, 1865, in Atlanta, Georgia (5-28-1864, 7-21-1864, 1-1-1865, 1-24-1865, 2-13-1865)

Grant, Ulysses S.: Born in Point Pleasant, Ohio, on April 27, 1822, he graduated from West Point in 1843. He became colonel of the Twenty-first Illinois Infantry in June of 1861, then brigadier general of volunteers. Following numerous tactical achievements throughout the Civil War, President Abraham Lincoln made Grant general-in-chief at a three-star rank in March 1863. He was U.S. president from1869 to 1877 and died of throat cancer in Mount McGregor, New York, on July 23, 1885. (5-30-1863, 1-15-1864)

Harris, Henry T.: At the age of thirty-three, this Indiana native and resident of Fairfield joined the Fourth Iowa Cavalry, Company M, on November 12, 1861. He made saddler on September 1, 1863, and was mustered out on May 13, 1865. (9-14-1863, 8-29-1864)

Howe, Samuel: At the age of thirty-four, this Canadian who was living in Mount Pleasant enlisted on February 14, 1862, in the Fourth Iowa Cavalry, Company M. He transferred to the Veteran Reserve Corps on August 9, 1865, and was discharged on August 29, 1865, at St. Louis, Missouri. He apparently was a close associate of Jacob Gantz during the war. (4-23-1863, 4-24-1863, 8-2-1863, 8-13-1863, 10-4-1863, 11-1-1863,

1-25-1864, 8-7-1864, 8-14-1864, 8-24-1864)

Kelly, John L.: A native of Ohio and resident of Birmingham, this twenty-six-year-old enlisted October 20, 1861, in the Fourth Iowa Cavalry, Company M. He was promoted to company quartermaster sergeant on January 1, 1864, and was mustered out on August 8, 1865, in Atlanta, Georgia. (Jacob Gantz mentions buying a record book in which to record his daily comments from John M. Kelly in the introduction to the book for 1863. It is believed that it was John L. Kelly.) (3-21-1865)

Kelly, Robert: On October 5, 1863, this nineteen-year-old native of Ohio and resident of Fairfield enlisted in the Fourth Iowa Cavalry, Company M. He was mustered out on August 8, 1865, in Atlanta, Georgia. (8-9-1864)

Kirkpatrick, Andrew J.: Ohio native and Mount Pleasant resident, Kirkpatrick, age forty-four, was promoted to chaplain from Company K of the Fourth Iowa Cavalry on November 29, 1861. Upon expiration of his term of service on December 5, 1864, he was discharged at Memphis, Tennessee. (4-5-1863)

Kirkpatrick, Samuel H.: He was twenty years old and living in Mount Pleasant when this native Iowan enlisted December 4, 1861. He was mustered out on August 8, 1865 in Atlanta, Georgia. (10-19-1863)

Lathers, James: At age thirty-three, this Jefferson County resident and Indiana native enlisted in the Fourth Iowa Cavalry on March 21, 1864. He was wounded with Jacob Gantz at Six-Mile Creek, Alabama, but is recorded as being mustered out at Atlanta, Georgia, on August 8, 1865. (4-1-1865)

Laughlin, William: This is believed to be a neighbor of the Gantzes near Brookville, Iowa. There is a Gantz-Laughlin family cemetery in Locust Grove Township, Jefferson County. (8-8-1863)

Lee, William B.: An Iowan from birth and resident of Mount Pleasant, Lee joined as a twenty-year-old in the Fourth Iowa Cavalry, Company M, on March 2, 1862. He was mustered out on August 8, 1865, in Atlanta, Georgia. (3-18-1863, 1-26-1865)

Logsdon, Albert W.: At age nineteen, this Ohio native and resident of Lockridge joined the Fourth Iowa Cavalry, on November 21, 1863. He died of disease at Hebron's Plantation near Vicksburg, Mississippi, on February 3, 1864. (2-3-1864)

Lowery, William: A native of Pennsylvania, this thirty-five-year-old was a resident of Fairfield when he joined the Fourth Iowa Cavalry on November 12, 1861. He was mustered out on December 5, 1864, in Memphis, Tennessee, upon completion of his term of service. (9-14-1863)

Lowman, Jacob: He was thirty-six years old when he enlisted on October 31, 1861. This native Pennsylvanian and resident of Lockridge died of disease on September 6, 1863, in the regimental hospital near Big Black River, Mississippi. (8-18-1863, 8-21-1863, 9-6-1863)

McConnaughey, Thomas: A resident of Rome and native of Ohio, this twenty-seven-year-old became bugler when he enlisted on October 10,

1861. He achieved the rank of 2d sergeant on May 1, 1864, and was mustered out at Atlanta, Georgia, on August 8, 1865. (2-21-1864)

McMurray, Thomas F.: This twenty-four-year-old, a native of Pennsylvania, was living at Lockridge when he enlisted in the Fourth Iowa Cavalry on October 22, 1861. He was promoted 3d corporal on May 1, 1864, and farrier on January 1, 1865, and was mustered out on August 8, 1865, in Atlanta, Georgia. (3-27-1863)

Majors, Alexander A.: At the age of twenty-one, this native Iowan and Mount Pleasant resident joined the Fourth Iowa Cavalry, Company M, on February 27, 1862. He was mustered out on August 8, 1865, at Atlanta, Georgia. He may also have served in the Fourteenth Infantry, Company E. (11-13-1863)

Marmaduke, Confederate Gen. John Sappington: He was born near Arrow Rock, Missouri, on March 14, 1833, and studied at Harvard and Yale before his appointment to West Point where he graduated thirtieth in a class of thirty-eight in 1857. He was promoted brigadier general on November 15, 1862, after distinguished service at Shiloh. He was captured at Mine Creek, Kansas, and was a prisoner of war at Fort Warren in Boston. After the war, he was in insurance and politics. He died while governor of Missouri on December 28, 1887. (10-25-1864)

Osterhaus, Gen. Peter Joseph: This was one of the most distinguished foreigners to achieve the rank of general in the Union army. He was a native of Prussia who went to military school in Berlin and came to the United States after serving in the revolutions in Europe. He was in business in Belleville and Lebanon, Illinois, and St. Louis, Missouri, before joining the Union cause. After the war, he was a U.S. diplomat in France and Germany. He died on January 2, 1917, and was buried in Germany. (6-16-1863, 7-9-1863)

Pemberton, Confederate Gen. John Clifford: Called the "Defender of Vicksburg," Pemberton was a native of Philadelphia, Pennsylvania, having been born there in August of 1814. He graduated from West Point where he had professed a deep love for the South. He resigned from the U.S. Army on April 24, 1861, and joined the Confederacy. He became lieutenant general in October 1862. He surrendered Vicksburg to Maj. Gen. U. S. Grant on July 4, 1863. After the war he settled on a farm near Warrenton, Virginia, and eventually returned to Pennsylvania where he died in July 1881. (1-15-1864)

Pleasonton, Gen. Alfred: Born in the District of Columbia on July 7, 1824, Pleasonton graduated seventh in the class of 1844 at the U.S. Military Academy. He was transferred to the Department of the Missouri, but was replaced as Cavalry Corps commander in March 1864 by Maj. Gen. Philip Sheridan. Embittered, Pleasonton resigned in January 1868 and died in Washington, D.C., on February 17, 1897. (10-21-1864)

Price, Confederate Gen. Sterling: He was born on September 20, 1809, in Prince Edward City, Virginia. He began his career in the Civil War by striving to keep Missouri for the Rebels—his main goal throughout the war. He had been a congressman and governor of that state prior to the war. He led the defeat of the Union army at Wilson Creek, Missouri, on August 10, 1861, and at Lexington, Missouri, ten days later. But those were his final victories. After the war, Price went to Mexico but returned to St. Louis, Missouri, in 1867 poor both in health and finances. He died there on September 29, 1867. (6-15-1863, 10-21-1864, 10-22-1864, 10-26-1864, 11-4-1864)

Riley, John Q.: He was a trumpeter for the Fourth Iowa Cavalry, Company E, when he was wounded with Jacob Gantz in Alabama. No other information was located about Riley. (4-1-1865)

Ripley, William: At the age of twenty-nine, this native of Maine and resident of Lockridge joined the Fourth Iowa Cavalry on October 23, 1861. He was mustered out at Atlanta, Georgia, on August 8, 1865. (8-1-1863)

Rowe, Gilbert: A resident of Rome and native of New York, this thirty-one-year-old enlisted on November 25, 1861, as company quartermaster sergeant for Company M of the Fourth Iowa Cavalry. On March 7, 1865, in Paducah, Kentucky, he died of disease and was buried in National Cemetery in Mound City, Illinois, Section E, grave 4,442. (4-5-1863, 10-16-1863, 5-1-1864)

Sheafor, Martin: At twenty-two, this Ohio native and Fairfield resident enlisted on November 12, 1861, in the Fourth Iowa Cavalry, Company M. He was promoted to 2d lieutenant on January 19, 1864, and was mustered out on August 8, 1865, in Atlanta, Georgia. (10-31-1863, 12-4-1863, 1-1-1864, 5-20-1864)

Sherman, Gen. William T.: Perhaps equally loved by the North and hated by the South, this Union general is best remembered for his march through Atlanta, Georgia, and on to the sea. He was a native of Ohio, attended West Point, and first fought in the Mexican War. He was a banker, lawyer, and military school superintendent in Louisiana. He rejected a commission in the Confederate army when the Civil War began and accepted an appointment as colonel in the federal army. He died in 1891. (6-16-1863)

Shoopman, Thomas H.: He was residing in Virginia in his native Illinois when he enlisted on November 22, 1861, in the Fourth Iowa Cavalry, Company M. On October 2, 1864, he died of disease in Keokuk, Iowa, at age twenty-four. (9-6-1863, 10-18-1863)

Skeers, Eli: This Pennsylvania native and resident of Mount Pleasant was forty-three when he joined the Fourth Iowa Cavalry, Company M, on March 2, 1862. He died of disease on November 16, 1864, in Jefferson County, Iowa. (8-9-1864)

Skeers, Jesse: A native of Iowa and resident of Lockridge, this twenty-year-old enlisted on October 23, 1861. He died of disease on August 2, 1863, in Bridgeport, Mississippi. (8-2-1863)

Smith, Gen. Giles Alexander: He was born in 1829 and died in 1876. Smith was in the dry-goods and hotel business when he became captain of the Eighth Missouri in June 1861. He was breveted major general on September 1, 1864, for the Atlanta and Savannah campaigns. He was mustered out in 1866. (10-21-1864)

Smith, Mother: This apparently was Jacob Gantz's mother-in-law. (8-25-1864)

Smith, William C.: He was twenty-one and residing in Jefferson County when he enlisted on March 21, 1864. This Pennsylvania native was mustered out on August 8, 1865, in Atlanta, Georgia. (1-26-1865)

Taylor, James H.: A resident of Glasgow and native of Iowa, this twenty-two-year-old enlisted in the Fourth Iowa Cavalry, Company M, on November 25, 1861. He was mustered out on August 8, 1865, in Atlanta, Georgia. (2-28-1865)

Thompson, David: At the age of thirty-eight, this Fairfield resident—a native of Scotland—enlisted on November 21, 1861, as 5th sergeant in the Fourth Iowa Cavalry, Company M. He became company commissary sergeant on January 1, 1864, and was mustered out at Atlanta, Georgia, on August 8, 1865. (8-1-1863)

Thompson, George: As a resident of Van Buren County and native of New York, this twenty-four-year-old enlisted on October 20, 1861, in the Fourth Iowa Cavalry, Company M. He was promoted to company commissary sergeant on October 1, 1862, reduced to 2d sergeant on January 1, 1864, and promoted to 1st sergeant on May 1, 1864, before being mustered out on August 8, 1865, in Atlanta, Georgia. (8-11-1863, 10-18-1863)

Turner, James I.: This eighteen-year-old Glasgow resident and Iowa native enlisted in the Fourth Iowa Cavalry, Company M, on November 2, 1861. He was mustered out on August 8, 1865, in Atlanta, Georgia. He may also have served in the Thirtieth Infantry, Company G. (11-18-1863)

Tuttle, James Madison: He was born in Summerfield, Ohio, in September 1823 but moved to Farmington, Iowa, as a young man. He was a farmer, merchant, sheriff, treasurer, and recorder of deeds in Van Buren County before joining the Second Iowa Infantry as lieutenant colonel on May 31, 1861. Because of alleged scandalous activities, Tuttle resigned on June 14, 1864, and returned to Iowa where he was a member of the state legislature after the war. He also was in real estate and the meat-packing business. He died in Casa Grande, Arizona, on October 24, 1892. (2-26-1864)

Uptagraft, Jacob: On November 2, 1861, this twenty-nine-year-old Fairfield resident and native of Pennsylvania enlisted in the Fourth Iowa Cavalry. He was taken prisoner in Helena, Arkansas, on September 30, 1862, but was exchanged on November 16, 1862. He was mustered out in Atlanta, Georgia, on August 8, 1865. (8-11-1863)

Vance, Daniel: At the age of twenty-one, this Salina resident and Indiana native enlisted in the Fourth Iowa Cavalry on October 22, 1861, as 1st sergeant. He was promoted to 1st lieutenant on January 19, 1864, and was mustered out in Atlanta, Georgia, on August 8, 1865. (2-6-1865)

Warner, Wilson: A resident of Libertyville and native of Ohio, this twenty-two-year-old enlisted in the Fourth Iowa Cavalry, Company M, on January 11, 1862, and was mustered out in Atlanta, Georgia, on August 8, 1865. (12-9-1863)

White, Samuel R.: This Pennsylvania native and Salina resident enlisted at age eighteen in the Fourth Iowa Cavalry, Company M, on October 22, 1861. He was taken prisoner on October 18, 1863, in Clinton, Mississippi, and died in Andersonville (Georgia) prison on September 25, 1864. (10-20-1863)

Whiting, Frederick: At age twenty-five, this Fairfield resident and Ohio native was appointed 1st lieutenant of the Fourth Iowa Cavalry, Company M, on November 2, 1861. He was promoted to captain on January 19, 1864, and was mustered out in Atlanta, Georgia, on August 8, 1864. (8-2-1863, 1-1-1864, 6-22-1864)

Wilcox, Phineas W.: A resident of Fairfield and native of Ohio, this twenty-six-year-old enlisted in the Fourth Iowa Cavalry on November 25, 1861. He was mustered out on December 5, 1864, upon expiration of his term of service. (3-26-1863, 3-8-1864, 5-9-1864)

Williams, William H. H.: On December 14, 1861, this Illinois native who was residing in Glasgow enlisted in the Fourth Iowa Cavalry, Company M. He was mustered out in Memphis, Tennessee, on December 5, 1864, upon completion of his term of service. He may also have served in Company G. (9-14-1863)

Wilson, Gen. James Harrison: Born near Shawneetown, Illinois, on September 2, 1837, Wilson was a West Point graduate who linked his service with U. S. Grant and became brigadier general on October 30, 1863. He outmaneuvered and outmarched Confederate Lt. Gen. Nathan Forrest in Alabama to take Selma on April 2, 1865. He became major general in June 1865, resigned in 1870, but reentered the service during the Spanish-American War until 1901. In civilian life, he was an engineer and railroad executive. He died in Wilmington, Delaware, as one of the last surviving Union generals on February 23, 1925. (3-7-1865)

Winslow, Gen. Edward Francis: He was born in 1937 and died in 1914. In April 1863, his Fourth Iowa Cavalry was the only cavalry regiment in Grant's army. He was wounded on May 12, 1863, at 14-Mile Creek, Mississippi, and was made brigadier general on December 12, 1864. He became a successful railroad builder and executive after the war. (10-21-1864, 2-2-1865, "After the War")

Woods, Mrs. M. E.: She was a well-to-do lady from Iowa who volunteered as a Union nurse during the Civil War. She went to the battlefields, not just to the hospitals, and she was appointed sanitary agent by the secretary of war on February 11, 1863. (10-26-1863, 10-27-1863, 10-28-1863)

Young, Robert: A native of Ireland but living in Salina, Young, age thirty-nine, enlisted as 1st corporal in the Fourth Iowa Cavalry, Company M, on

October 22, 1861. He was promoted to 3d sergeant on December 5, 1864, and mustered out at Atlanta, Georgia, on August 8, 1865. (8-1-1863, 9-1-1863)

Significant Dates

April 4, 1863: Medical records in the National Archives, Washington, D.C., indicate that Jacob Gantz was treated for a fever on this date at the regimental hospital.

July 10, 1863: Jacob Gantz first mentions a boil under his arm, but he apparently was not treated for this problem for six more weeks.

August 22, 1863: Treatment for the boil under his arm was reported in medical records on Jacob Gantz obtained from the National Archives. He was admitted at the regimental hospital and returned to duty the following day.

December 11, 1863: Military records in the National Archives indicate that Jacob Gantz reenlisted on this day.

March 4, 1864: Jacob Gantz talks about starting for home on this date and writes about the travel upstream through March 17, 1864. Both the company muster roll and pension records obtained from the National Archives said he was on sick leave in Iowa from March through April 1864. Gantz, on the other hand, said he went home on veteran's furlough.

May 1, 1864: Military records indicate that Jacob Gantz was promoted to 5th corporal on this day. He was en route to his regiment after his furlough.

June 24, 1864: In the military records and on his application for pension following the service, both from the National Archives, it is noted that Jacob Gantz was on a scouting expedition at this time.

September 2, 1864: Again on his military and pension records, it is noted that Jacob Gantz was on an expedition at this time.

January 1, 1865: Military records on file at the National Archives indicate that Jacob Gantz was promoted to 3d corporal on this day.

February 9, 1865: Jacob Gantz mentions that he has sore eyes, but the regiment is on a boat headed for Alabama on the Ohio and Tennessee rivers and he apparently does not receive treatment immediately. For the next several days his writing and spelling worsens as he continues to mention the pain he is suffering in his eyes. He mentions that many others in Company M are suffering with sore eyes.

February 15, 1865: Medical records from the National Archives indicate that Jacob Gantz was treated for ophthalmia on this date. By February 18, 1865, Gantz notes that his eyes are much improved.

April 1, 1865: Jacob Gantz mentions the wounded with him in general terms. In "The Story of a Cavalry Regiment" (p. 572), those listed as wounded at Six-Mile Creek on March 31, 1865, included Gantz, Company M pvts. Villeroy Abbey, Oliver F. Chester, and James Lathers. Also wounded there was Company E trumpeter John Q. Riley.

NOTES

Introduction

1. *Portrait and Biographical Album of Prominent Citizens in Jefferson and Van Buren Counties*, 327.
2. Ibid.
3. Ibid., 328.
4. *Roster and Register of Iowa Soldiers in the War of the Rebellion*, vol. 4, 639.
5. Ibid., 640.
6. James M. McPherson, *Battle Cry of Freedom*, 326.
7. *Roster and Register of Iowa Soldiers in the War of the Rebellion*, vol. 4, 641.
8. Ibid.
9. Ibid., 643.
10. Paul E. Steiner, *Disease in the Civil War*, 10.
11. Ibid., 11.
12. Jacob G. Forman, *The Western Sanitary Commission*, 142.
13. *Portrait and Biographical Album of Prominent Citizens in Jefferson and Van Buren Counties*, 328.

III: After the War

1. *Roster and Register of Iowa Soldiers in the War of the Rebellion*, vol. 4, 660.
2. Ibid., 661.
3. Frederick Dyer, *A Compendium of the War of the Rebellion*, vol. 1.
4. Jacob S. Gantz, medical records, National Archives, Washington, D.C.
5. Jacob S. Gantz, pension records, National Archives, Washington, D.C.
6. *Portrait and Biographical Album of Prominent Citizens in Jefferson and Van Buren Counties*, 327.
7. Genealogical records, Fairfield Public Library, Fairfield, Iowa.
8. *History of Jefferson County, 1879*, Chicago: Western Historical Co., 1879, 469.

9.   *Portrait and Biographical Album of Prominent Citizens in Jefferson and Van Buren Counties,* 327. (The exact location of The Gantz House was determined with the assistance of Jefferson County genealogist Verda Baird, using my tidbits of information and her vast knowledge of the city's history.)
10. Ibid. 328.
11. Genealogical records, Fairfield Public Library, Fairfield, Iowa.
12. *Portrait and Biographical Album of Prominent Citizens in Jefferson and Van Buren Counties,* 328.
13. Genealogical records, Fairfield Public Library, Fairfield, Iowa.
14. Fairfield *Daily Ledger,* February 21, 1942, "Looking Backward—Thirty years ago."
15. Fairfield *Daily Ledger,* February 21, 1942, "Looking Backward—Twenty years ago."

BIBLIOGRAPHY

Dyer, Frederick. *A Compendium of the War of the Rebellion*, vol. 1. New York: Yoseloff, 1959.

English, E. A.. *Roster and Register of Iowa Soldiers in the War of the Rebellion*, vol. 4. Des Moines, Iowa, 1908.

Esposito, Vincent J., ed. *The West Point Atlas of American Wars*, vol. 1. New York: Praeger, 1959.

Fairfield *Daily Ledger*, February 21, 1942.

Forman, Jacob G. *The Western Sanitary Commission*, published for the Mississippi Valley Sanitary Fair. St. Louis: R. P. Studley and Co., 1864.

Genealogy records, various sources collected by the Jefferson County Genealogy Society, available at the Fairfield Public Library, Fairfield, Iowa.

History of Jefferson County. Chicago: Western Historical Co., 1879.

McPherson, James M. *Battle Cry of Freedom*. New York: Oxford University Press, 1988.

National Archives, Jacob Gantz's medical, military, and pension records. Washington, D.C.

Portrait and Biographical Album of Prominent Citizens in Jefferson and Van Buren Counties. Chicago: Lake City Publishing Co., 1890.

Steiner, Paul E. *Disease in the Civil War*. Springfield, Ill.: Charles C. Thomas Publ., 1968.

INDEX

Reconnoitering force
  one-hundred-mile trek, 66
  scouting trips, 57
Recruiting, at home, 43
Rheumatism, 9
Roads, poor condition of, 50
Roasting ears (corn), 66
Rock, Margaret Vance, 100
Rural enlistees, and incidence of
  illness, 8

Saber, presented to Col. Edward
  Winslow, 85
St. Patrick, 80
Sanitary Commission, 10
Sanitary goods
  in Alabama, 88
  received, 21
  spoilage, 29
Satarshia, Miss., 29
Scout, searching for Confederate
  general Nathan Forrest, 60
Scurvy, 9
Selma, Ala., 91
Sherman, William T., 33
Sleep, lack of, 63
Smallpox, 9
Smith, Giles A., 74
Snow, first experienced in the South,
  49
Sorrow, reasons for, 11
South Carolina, first state to secede, 3
Southern heat, effect on troops, 8
Sowbelly, meal on scout, 59
Spencer carbines, 62, 65
Spy, Fourth Iowa Cavalry among
  Rebels, 33
Star of the West, 3
Sunstroke, 9, 29
Syphilis, 9
Sypsey, stream in Alabama, 89

Talbot's Ferry, Ark., 8
Tennessee River, icy conditions, 86
Third Iowa Cavalry

battle at Independence, Mo., 75
casualty, 64
leaving Kentucky, 84
visiting, 68, 70, 84
Tenth Missouri, leaving for Alabama,
  84
Tonsillitis, 9
Train, escorting forage loads, 27, 34, 51
Travel, 8
Troops
  need for blankets, 7
  swing, 11
Truce
  exchange of sick prisoners, 69
  Port Hudson, surrendered, 31
Tuberculosis, 9
Typhoid, 9

Veterans
  enlistment, 45
  news about going home, 50
Vicksburg, Miss.
  after the battle, 37
  elements for success, 17
  heavy firing, 27
  mail service, 11
  moving toward, 26
  river and bayou system, 17
  surrender of, 18, 32, 33
  tree rings made of surrender
    location, 50
  trip for supplies, 52
  Union forces advance, 24
  Union strategy, 18
  victory celebration, 11, 32
Voting, presidential election of 1864,
  11, 78

Water, scarce supply, 33
Waterloo, Ala., Fourth Iowa Cavalry
  arrives, 85, 86
Watermelon, local produce, 70
Weapons, seized, 76
Weather
  freezing temperatures, 39